BEFORE THE LOSS

Because Grief Is Hard Enough

PAUL FRIED

MILTON & HUGO L.L.C.
1001 3rd Avenue West, Suite 430
Bradenton, FL 34205, USA

Website: *www. miltonandhugo.com*
Hotline: *1- 888-778-0033*
Email: *info@miltonandhugo.com*

Ordering Information:
Quantity sales. Special discounts are granted to corporations, associations, and other organizations. For more information on these discounts, please reach out to the publisher using the contact information provided above.

Library of Congress Control Number: 2026902796
ISBN-13:   979-8-89285-803-8   [Paperback Edition]
                  979-8-89285-807-6   [Hardback Edition]
                  979-8-89285-804-5   [Digital Edition]

Rev. date: 02/04/2026

CONTENTS

Preface

Every person who picks up this book has experienced loss or will experience it. Grief is not an experience reserved for a few. It comes for all of us. It arrives quietly or violently. It arrives expected or unexpected. It arrives in ways that change the structure of our lives forever.

Yet even though grief is universal, few of us know how to move through it. We stumble in the dark. We struggle to find our way. The pain is heavy enough on its own, yet it becomes far heavier when confusion is added to the moment. When someone we love dies, we are handed responsibilities we are not emotionally ready to carry. We are asked to make decisions when our hearts are breaking. We are asked to solve problems we never discussed. We are asked to act when we can barely breathe.

The truth I have learned is that grief becomes harder when families are left without clarity. The emotional strain increases. The chaos grows. The arguments begin. The guilt deepens. These are the moments that tear people apart. These are the moments that can be prevented.

I wrote this book because I believe families deserve better. They deserve guidance. They deserve support. They deserve a roadmap at a time when nothing feels stable. They deserve clarity instead of chaos and peace instead of panic.

This book is not about removing grief. Nothing can or should remove grief. It is the expression of love. This book is about reducing the stress that surrounds it. It is about preparing families for the hardest day of their lives so they can face it with strength and unity rather than fear and confusion.

Author's Note

I never expected my life to lead me into end-of-life planning, but in many ways, it has been there from the beginning. Long before I built a platform or wrote a word about grief, I understood, sometimes quietly, sometimes uncomfortable, that what we leave behind matters.

My father was a Holocaust survivor. His life was shaped by experiences most of us cannot imagine; and yet he went on to build a family grounded in discipline, humility, gratitude, and generosity. What he endured taught me resilience. What he didn't speak about taught me something else, that when important conversations are avoided, the weight of them often falls on the next generation.

When he died, I realized how much we had never talked about. There were questions I didn't ask and details that were never clarified. That absence stayed with me. It made me think deeply about what it means to care for the people we love, not just while we're here but in what we leave behind.

For much of my professional life, I was a builder. I built houses. I built buildings. And I know this to be true—nothing gets built successfully, or efficiently, without a clear plan. You don't pour a foundation without blueprints. You don't frame a structure without knowing where it's going. Without a plan, projects stall, costs rise, and mistakes multiply.

Yet when it comes to death, funerals, and final wishes, we live in a culture that avoids planning altogether.

We are deeply uncomfortable talking about death. We postpone it. We deny it. We tell ourselves we'll get to it later.

But dying and funerals are not abstract ideas, they are life-cycle events. They are as inevitable as birth and as human as love. When we refuse to talk about them, we don't eliminate stress; we pass it on to the people we care about most.

What I've come to understand is that much of the hardship families experience after a loss isn't caused by grief itself. Grief is natural. It's the confusion, the unanswered questions, the rushed decisions, and the financial and logistical uncertainty that create unnecessary suffering. When there is no plan, families are forced to navigate some of life's hardest moments under pressure, often while emotionally overwhelmed.

Planning changes that.

Having a plan doesn't diminish emotion; it protects it. It allows families to grieve naturally and freely, without the added burden of trying to guess what their loved one would have wanted or scrambling to manage details in the midst of loss. Clarity creates space for compassion. Preparation is an act of care.

I created *I Made the Arrangements* because I believe planning is not about control; it's about responsibility. It's about love expressed in advance. It's about leaving guidance instead of silence and peace instead of chaos.

This book grows out of that belief. It isn't about avoiding grief. It's about minimizing the avoidable stress that so often surrounds it. It's written for people who want to take responsibility for their life-cycle planning and give their families the gift of clarity when it matters most.

Thank you for being here. My hope is that this work encourages more open conversations, more thoughtful preparation, and a shift in how we approach one of the most universal, and most avoided, parts of being human.

Chapter 1

WHY WE DO NOT TALK ABOUT DEATH

We live in a world where people talk freely about almost everything. We debate politics and argue about sports. We post opinions about news and entertainment. We talk about parenting and relationships and the stress of daily life. We talk about what we want to achieve and where we want to travel. We talk about diet and health and what we will do next weekend. Yet there is one subject that remains largely untouched: death.

Not because it is rare. Not because it is complicated. We avoid it because it is final. It forces us to confront the reality that our time is limited. It forces us to imagine losing the people we love. It forces us to acknowledge that life is unpredictable and that control is more fragile than we like to admit. For many people, the easiest way to deal with that discomfort is not to deal with it at all. We change the subject. We make jokes. We say, "Let's not go there." We push the thought away and tell ourselves we will handle it later.

But our silence around death is not simply personal. It is cultural. It is inherited. Generations have passed it down as if talking about death were dangerous. Some people worry that naming it invites it, as if the mere act of speaking could pull tragedy closer. Others avoid it because they believe it will upset someone or because they do not want to "ruin the moment."

Many hold onto the quiet superstition that if they push death out of their minds long enough, it will somehow take care of itself. Yet silence does not protect us. Silence leaves us unprepared. Silence creates suffering for the families who remain.

There was a time when death was a visible part of life. People died at home, surrounded by family. Children saw the process. Families sat vigil. Rituals were intimate and familiar. Death was understood because it was witnessed. Over time, that changed. Death moved out of the home. Hospitals and institutions took over. What once happened in the center of family life began to happen behind closed doors. It became something clinical and distant, something managed by professionals and hidden from daily experience. When people stopped seeing death, they stopped processing it. When they stopped processing it, they stopped speaking about it. Our discomfort grew because death became a stranger.

As death became hidden, daily life became more sanitized. We placed illness and aging at the edges of society. We praised youth. We celebrated productivity. Death no longer fit into the picture we wanted to paint. It became an interruption rather than a natural chapter of life. This shift brought consequences. When people do not see death, they do not understand it. When people do not understand it, they do not prepare for it. When people do not prepare, suffering reaches the next generation.

Part of what makes death so hard to face is that it threatens a powerful illusion: the belief that life is something we can manage fully. We plan everything. We schedule appointments. We create budgets. We pick schools and careers. We make lists. We spend our lives organizing and hoping structure will keep the unpredictable away. Death ignores structure. It arrives on its own timeline. It does not ask permission. Because of that, most people push the subject aside. Pretending it is far away feels easier than acknowledging that it can arrive without warning.

There is a strange irony here. True control does not come from avoiding death. It comes from acknowledging it. Preparing for death is not giving up. It is claiming agency. It is choosing clarity over fear. People who document their wishes often feel lighter afterward, as if they have put down a weight they did not realize they were carrying. They move through life with a sense of readiness. They know they have protected their families in a way that matters deeply. Control is not the power to prevent death. Control is the ability to ease the burden your death will place on the people who love you.

Because grief itself, as painful as it is, is natural. It is the expression of love. The deeper the love, the deeper the ache. What makes grief unbearable for many families is not the loss alone, but the confusion and responsibility that immediately follow. A grieving family is suddenly expected to make decisions that should have been made long before. They must select a funeral home. They must choose between burial and cremation. They must write an obituary. They must determine who to call and what to say. They must gather documents they cannot find. They must locate financial accounts and passwords and insurance policies. All of this happens at the exact moment their emotions are at their weakest. They are asked to think clearly at a time when thinking clearly is almost impossible.

I recall meeting a woman who had lost her husband unexpectedly. They had been married for more than forty years. He had handled most of the paperwork. When he died, she was not only heartbroken, but she was also terrified. She had no idea where anything was kept. She did not know their passwords. She could not locate important documents. She felt lost, and she felt guilty. She believed she had failed him simply because she did not know what he had never explained. In contrast, I once knew a man who prepared everything before he died. He left detailed plans. He organized his accounts. He wrote letters. He documented his wishes clearly. When he passed, his family cried with grief and gratitude at the same time. They felt held. They felt guided. They felt loved. His preparation removed chaos. It created clarity, and that clarity became its own form of comfort. The difference between those two families was not love. It was preparation.

Another reason people avoid talking about death is that they believe discussing it removes hope. They worry that planning implies surrender. Yet the opposite is often true. When someone nearing the end of their life begins speaking openly about their wishes, a transformation can occur. It creates connection. It reduces fear. It clears the emotional fog that silence has created. Families who avoid the conversation experience a different outcome. They dance around the truth. They pretend everything is fine. They hide their fear from one another. The result is emotional distance at the exact time closeness is needed most. Silence becomes heavy. It creates tension instead of easing it. Talking about death does not erase hope. It replaces fear with honesty. It strengthens relationships rather than weakening them.

People also misunderstand who benefits most from planning. They believe planning is for themselves. In truth, planning is for the people who will carry the emotional weight long after they are gone. The person who dies does not face the paperwork. They do not face the phone calls. They do not organize the funeral arrangements. They do not argue with family members about what should happen next. All of that falls on the shoulders of the living.

When someone creates a clear plan, they protect their loved ones from an emotional avalanche. They remove the burden of guesswork. They prevent arguments. They prevent guilt. They prevent that awful moment when someone asks what their loved one would have wanted and no one knows the answer. *I Made the Arrangements* was built to solve this problem. The purpose was not to create another digital tool. The purpose was to create a pathway that makes planning feel simple and accessible. Many people never start planning because they believe it requires an attorney or complicated paperwork. But most of what families need can be documented clearly with a few straightforward questions: a funeral plan, a will, an advance directive, account information, legacy messages. These do not require legal training. They require thoughtfulness. They require honesty. They require a willingness to face the truth and protect the people left behind.

The tools inside *I Made the Arrangements* guide users gently. They reduce the fear that surrounds planning. They turn a heavy subject into something manageable. When people complete their plan, they often express a profound sense of relief. They no longer carry the unspoken worry of what will happen when they die. They know their family will not face chaos. They know they have done something meaningful. Planning becomes an act of love. It becomes a final gift.

If avoidance is human nature, it is also true that avoidance comes with a cost. Human beings naturally avoid what makes them anxious. It is part of our biology. When a subject creates discomfort, the mind pushes it aside. The problem is that avoidance does not reduce anxiety. It intensifies it. The longer we avoid something, the larger it becomes in our mind. The fear grows quietly in the background, shaping our lives even when we pretend it is not there.

Clarity has the opposite effect. When people confront the subject of death directly, they do not become more afraid. They often become calmer. They understand the emotional landscape better. They feel prepared. Even small steps, such as discussing funeral preferences, can reduce anxiety. The unknown is far more frightening than the known. Families are more resilient when expectations are defined. The human brain copes better when it knows what to expect. Planning gives the brain structure, and structure brings calm in moments of turmoil. When guidance is clear after a death, families argue less. They carry less trauma. They recover more naturally. Their grief is still deep, but it is not complicated by crisis management. Clarity allows grief to be grief.

People often ask how to start talking about death with their loved ones. They imagine the conversation must be somber and heavy and filled with sadness. But the conversation is often filled with relief. When one person breaks the silence, the tension dissolves. People exhale. Fear loses its edge. A conversation about death does not need to be dramatic. It can begin with a simple thought. It can begin with a question. It can begin with a story about someone else and how their family struggled, or how they found comfort. The important part is that the conversation begins. Once it does, comfort grows. Families who talk openly about death build stronger emotional connections because they build trust. They understand one another more deeply.

I have seen families who never talked about death finally sit together and share their thoughts. What follows is often gratitude and intimacy. The burden each person has been carrying in silence becomes lighter when spoken aloud. These conversations create a sense of unity that carries into the days and months after a loss.

We are living in a time when people are finally beginning to rethink their relationship with death. More people are exploring end-of-life doulas. More people are seeking information on funerals and legal documents. More people are realizing that ignoring death does not delay it. They recognize that planning is not a morbid act but a practical one and a profoundly loving one. This cultural shift is slow yet meaningful. It reflects a growing desire for authenticity and openness. People are tired of pretending that everything is fine when something is clearly not fine. They are tired of carrying unspoken fears. They are tired of the emotional burden that silence creates.

People want peace. People want connection. People want clarity, and they are beginning to understand that talking about death honestly is one of the most direct paths to those things.

At the end of life, every person leaves something behind. It may be love. It may be memories. It may be confusion. It may be chaos. The question is never whether we will leave something. The question is what shape it will take. Will our family be left with unanswered questions? Will they argue because they each remember our wishes differently? Will they struggle to find important documents? Will they feel guilty because they are uncertain about the decisions they made on our behalf? Or will we leave them with clarity? Will they feel supported? Will they know exactly what we wanted? Will they be able to grieve without being pulled into crisis mode?

Death is unavoidable. Chaos is not. Confusion is not. Emotional strain caused by lack of preparation is not. We cannot remove the pain of loss, but we can remove the suffering that comes from uncertainty.

This book is an invitation. It invites readers to face the truth with courage. It invites families to protect one another. It invites people to recognize that planning ahead is not about expecting death. It is about respecting life. It is about acknowledging that our decisions today can spare the people we love tomorrow.

The silence around death begins to end here. In the chapters that follow, we will examine the stress that grief creates. We will explore the way unprepared families suffer. We will look closely at the emotional and psychological consequences of avoidance and the transformative power of planning. We will identify the steps that bring peace of mind and the steps that reduce chaos.

We cannot choose when we die. But we can choose what we leave behind. We can choose love. We can choose clarity. We can choose comfort. When the time comes, the people we love most will feel the difference.

Chapter 2

THE HIDDEN STRESS OF GRIEF

Grief is often described as an emotional wound, yet it is far more complex than that. It is physical. It is mental. It is spiritual. It affects sleep and appetite. It alters memory and concentration. When someone loses a person they love, the entire body responds. Muscles tighten. Breathing changes. The nervous system shifts into survival mode. Thoughts become scattered. Everyday tasks become difficult. Even simple decisions can feel overwhelming.

Most people expect grief to be sadness, but sadness is only one piece. Grief is shock. It is confusion. It is fear. It is disorientation. It is the sudden disruption of a life that once felt predictable. Grief strips away the sense of stability people rely on. Nothing feels familiar. Nothing feels organized. It becomes hard to think clearly because the mind is trying to process an emotional impact that has no map. Grief is heavy, but there is a hidden truth many people discover only after loss: Grief itself is rarely what breaks someone. What breaks people is the stress that surrounds it.

When someone dies, the world does not pause. The phones keep ringing. The bills arrive. The decisions pile up. Families must choose a funeral home. They must review documents. They must notify employers. They must deal with insurance. They must coordinate with relatives. They must answer endless questions. All of this happens when the mind is least capable of processing information. People often describe this period as being inside a fog. They move through tasks mechanically. They forget facts. They repeat conversations. They feel as if they are floating outside their own life, and yet they are expected to perform at a time when performance is nearly impossible.

This collision between grief and responsibility is where hidden stress begins. The emotional brain and the decision-making brain cannot operate at full capacity at the same time. When grief overwhelms the emotional system, cognitive processing slows down. It becomes difficult to interpret information or make rational choices. Yet this is the exact moment society demands clarity and action. That mismatch between emotional capacity and practical demands creates immense hidden stress, and most grieving people blame themselves for it. They think something is wrong with them when in reality their brain is doing what it was designed to do in the face of shock.

There is a term used in psychology called widow brain. It describes the cognitive fog that often follows the death of a spouse. But this fog is not limited to widows. Almost anyone who experiences significant loss can go through a period of cognitive disruption. The brain is processing emotional trauma while attempting to function normally, and those two processes compete for the same resources. People in early grief struggle to remember appointments. They lose track of days. They forget conversations. They misplace objects. They find it difficult to focus on tasks that were once automatic. This is not a failure of discipline. It is a natural neurological response to loss.

At the same time, they are expected to make decisions with long-term consequences. They must interpret legal documents. They must authorize cremation or burial. They must select caskets or urns. They must sign contracts with funeral homes. They must manage financial accounts. The brain is rarely equipped to handle that level of cognitive load during grief, and the strain of trying to do it anyway becomes its own kind of suffering.

As if that were not enough, grief does not land in a vacuum. It lands inside families, inside relationships, inside old patterns. When a family is grieving, emotions run high. People who normally communicate well may become short-tempered. People who avoid conflict may suddenly become argumentative. Siblings who share the same childhood memories may disagree about what a parent wanted. Spouses may clash over choices that feel deeply emotional and deeply symbolic. These conflicts do not arise because people lack love. They arise because everyone is under strain, because everyone is attempting to interpret unspoken wishes, and because the emotional climate is volatile while the stakes feel enormous. One sibling may view cremation as appropriate. Another may view it as disrespectful. One partner may want a traditional funeral. The other may remember a casual conversation suggesting something entirely different. In the absence of a clear plan, relationships can become pressure cookers. Hidden stress builds inside the silence left behind.

Uncertainty is one of the most powerful stressors humans experience. When people are unsure what to do, they become anxious. When they feel responsible for honoring the wishes of someone they love, that anxiety intensifies. Uncertainty forces people to guess. Guessing creates guilt. Guilt becomes an emotional weight carried long after the funeral is over. Uncertainty also slows decision-making. People hesitate. They question themselves. They revisit choices repeatedly. The delay prolongs the administrative tasks that must be completed and extends the period of heightened stress. What could have been resolved in minutes with clear guidance can take months, sometimes years, when families are left to assemble the puzzle on their own. Uncertainty is not just confusing; it is emotionally exhausting. It is one of the hidden forces that makes grief feel heavier than it needs to be.

Stress does not stay in the mind. It moves into the body. People who are grieving often experience headaches and stomach pain. Sleep becomes disrupted. The immune system weakens. Muscles tense. Breathing becomes shallow. Blood pressure rises. Heart rate increases. These symptoms are not random. They are the body's response to overload. When grief is combined with planning and decision-making demands, the stress becomes more intense. People may skip meals without realizing it. Others may overeat in an attempt to calm the nervous system. Some feel restless. Others feel paralyzed. The body tries to manage what the mind cannot fully process. When tasks and responsibilities pile up at the same time, the physical toll grows heavier, which is why clear planning done in advance matters so much. It reduces the number of decisions being made during one of the most physically vulnerable periods of a person's emotional life.

The days and weeks after a death also bring an administrative storm that most people never see coming. Banks must be notified. Insurance companies must be contacted. Subscriptions must be cancelled. Employers must be informed. Digital accounts must be accessed. Legal documents must be located. Property must be sorted. Financial responsibilities must be transferred. These tasks may sound straightforward in theory. In practice, they become overwhelming because they occur during emotional and cognitive overload. Without a clear roadmap, people do not know where to start. They spend hours searching through old files or trying to guess passwords. They call companies and wait on hold. They repeat the same story again and again, reopening the wound each time. The tasks accumulate quickly. They demand mental energy at a time when mental energy is depleted. They demand patience at a time when patience feels impossible. They demand organization at a time when the mind is scattered. A clear plan reduces the administrative storm before it begins. Families know where to go and what to do. The logistical stress lifts, and grief does not have to compete with crisis management.

In many families, one person carries most of the household responsibilities. They manage the paperwork. They pay the bills. They store the documents. They make the financial decisions. When that person dies, responsibility shifts suddenly to someone who may have little experience managing those tasks. This shift creates enormous hidden stress. People feel unprepared. They feel overwhelmed. They feel as if they have been handed a job without training, and it is not simply a practical challenge. It is an emotional one. The weight of responsibility lands at the exact moment someone is already compromised by grief. When a plan exists, the transition becomes manageable. The surviving family member can follow clear directions rather than starting from scratch. Instead of digging through years of paperwork, they can access organized information. Instead of guessing, they can lean on certainty. That allows them to focus on healing.

Decision-making requires mental clarity, yet the early stages of grief are often marked by confusion and shock. People describe feeling detached from their surroundings. Time moves strangely. Information does not "stick." Choices get made and then forgotten. This emotional state is not compatible with major decisions that must be made after a death. Funeral arrangements are one example. These decisions are deeply personal and often expensive. They involve symbolic meaning and cultural significance. Without guidance, families may choose options that do not reflect the wishes of the person who died. They may also feel pressure from funeral directors, from relatives, or from the urgency of the moment. Legal matters require careful thought as well. People must navigate wills, trust documents, property transfers, and financial accounts. Mistakes made during this time can have lasting consequences.

When decisions are made in a state of grief, the risk of regret increases. People look back months or years later and question themselves. They wonder if they did the right thing. They replay conversations. They carry the weight of responsibility as if it were proof that they failed. That regret can deepen the pain of the loss. Clear planning removes this burden. Decisions can be made ahead of time when the mind is clear and emotions are steadier. That prevents regret and reduces the psychological stress grief can create.

This is why planning reduces hidden stress. Planning removes uncertainty, and when uncertainty is removed, stress decreases. People feel more grounded when they know what to expect. They feel calmer when they have clear direction. They feel supported when the logistical burden is lighter. Planning also reduces conflict. Families do not need to argue about preferences that were never discussed. They do not need to interpret vague memories of conversations. They do not need to guess. The plan becomes the guide, and everyone has something to follow.

Planning also shortens the administrative process. Documents can be accessed quickly. Accounts are listed clearly. Tasks are organized. Families can complete what needs to be done without unnecessary struggle. Most importantly, planning allows grief to be grief. When logistics are simplified, emotional space becomes larger. People have room to process feelings. They have room to support one another. They have room to mourn without being pulled into crisis mode.

Preparation does not remove the pain of losing someone you love. Nothing can. The true purpose of preparation is to reduce the avoidable suffering that surrounds loss. It is to give families a sense of order at a time of emotional chaos. It is to provide clarity where there would otherwise be confusion. It is to create structure in the midst of uncertainty. Preparation is a gift that extends beyond documents and details. It is a gesture of love that says, "I want to protect you from as much stress as possible." It is a gesture of compassion that says, "I want your grief to be uncomplicated." It is a gesture of responsibility that says, "I understand what I do today will shape how you experience tomorrow."

That is why *I Made the Arrangements* was created: to provide a pathway that reduces hidden stress, supports families, and transforms the experience of loss by replacing uncertainty with clarity. Grief is inevitable. Chaos is not. Confusion is not. Emotional overload is not. When people prepare thoughtfully, they create peace. They create stability. They create the conditions for healing. That is the hidden truth behind planning. It is not about death; it is about love. It is about easing the burden for the people who will carry the weight of your absence. It is about choosing clarity over chaos and compassion over avoidance. It is one of the most meaningful acts a person can offer the people they care about.

Chapter 3

HOW CONFUSION
COMPOUNDS PAIN

Grief on its own is powerful; but it is also, in a strange way, manageable. It is painful yet natural. It has a rhythm shaped by memory and love. People cry. People reflect. People lean on one another. With time, the sharpness softens, and the heart begins to adapt. The loss never disappears, but the mind learns how to carry it.

But when confusion enters the experience, grief becomes something else. It becomes heavier. It becomes unpredictable. It becomes tangled. Confusion disrupts the natural path of mourning and replaces it with emotional tension and psychological strain. It introduces questions with no immediate answers. It creates frustration at a time when patience is already thin. It creates doubt, and then guilt, and then the kind of emotional noise that overwhelms the mind. This is what transforms grief into complicated grief. Complicated grief is not deeper love. It is grief weighed down by chaos.

When someone dies without leaving direction, families are left with questions that pierce straight through the fog. What did they want for their final arrangements? What were their wishes? Did they have preferences? Did they share those preferences with someone else? Should the funeral be simple or elaborate? Should it be religious or secular? Who should speak? Where should it be held? Each question becomes a point of emotional stress, because these questions are never merely practical. They are symbolic. They feel like acts of loyalty. People fear getting the answer wrong. They fear choosing something the person would not have wanted. They fear letting them down.

That fear intensifies grief. It transforms sadness into anxiety. It transforms sorrow into pressure. It transforms natural emotion into emotional strain. Confusion forces people to dig through memories searching for clues. It makes them question conversations that happened years ago. It makes them debate the meaning behind remarks that were never intended as instructions. It forces them to interpret silence and call it direction. This is the hidden stress that complicates grief, not because families are doing something wrong but because they are trying to honor someone they loved without the map they needed.

Guessing becomes its own burden. Every guess feels like a risk, and every risk feels personal. People want certainty, but certainty does not exist when nothing has been documented. They feel alone inside the decision. They feel the weight of responsibility pressing down on them. Some people guess quickly because they have no energy left to agonize over another choice. Others become paralyzed by indecision, unable to move forward without reassurance that never comes. Neither path brings comfort. Both paths leave emotional residue that lingers long after the funeral has ended.

Months or years later, people remember the decisions they made. They wonder if they honored their loved one properly. They replay moments of uncertainty. They question themselves. That self-questioning becomes a quiet internal ache that complicates healing. Grief should not require guesswork. Guesswork belongs to situations with low stakes. Death is not one of those situations. When guesswork surrounds grief, confusion becomes part of the loss itself.

Confusion rarely stays contained within one person. It spreads throughout a family. It creates differences of opinion that can quickly escalate into conflict. People who normally communicate calmly may become defensive. People who avoid confrontation may suddenly speak with urgency. People interpret silence differently. They interpret memories differently. They interpret the wishes of the person who died differently. This is not because families lack love; it is because they lack clarity. Everyone is trying to do the right thing without knowing what the right thing is. Each person believes they are honoring the loved one. Each person believes their interpretation is accurate. Each person believes their responsibility is to protect the memory of the one they lost.

The tension that grows from this uncertainty can spark arguments that deepen the pain of the moment. Those arguments rarely disappear after the funeral. They linger. They resurface in later conversations. They become part of the emotional landscape of the family. Confusion is a quiet architect of conflict. It builds tension from nothing. It creates emotional fractures that can take years to heal. It complicates grief by adding relational strain to an already fragile time.

That is why clear wishes are so powerful. Human beings crave direction when facing something overwhelming. Direction settles the mind. It quiets anxiety. It creates a path to follow when the emotional world is turbulent. When wishes are documented, families feel anchored. They may still cry. They may still feel shock and sadness, but they do not feel lost. They do not feel pressured to interpret silence. They do not feel responsible for creating meaning out of uncertainty.

Clear wishes remove the emotional burden of decision-making. They remove the responsibility of being the one who must decide. They transform a moment of confusion into a moment of guidance. When someone provides their family with clear instructions, they give them a gift: certainty during one

17

of the most uncertain experiences of life. They give them relief during a moment when relief feels impossible. They reduce the emotional weight. They remove the confusion. They allow grief to be grief, rather than grief woven with fear.

Because in the hours and days following a death, families are expected to solve a series of logistical problems. These problems require focus and clarity, yet focus and clarity are weakened by emotional shock. People must select a funeral home. They must schedule services. They must make choices that are emotionally charged and financially significant. They must organize transportation. They must notify relatives who live far away. They must coordinate details they have never handled before. These tasks arrive at the exact moment emotional capacity is at its lowest. The heart is in pain, yet the world demands efficiency. People say they feel as if they are moving through water. Every action feels heavier than it should. Every conversation feels harder than it normally would. Every decision feels like a test they are afraid to fail.

Confusion magnifies this experience. Without clear direction, each task feels like a guess. Without a plan, every choice requires debate. Without guidance, each step requires interpretation. Logistics become emotionally loaded rather than simply procedural, and that added layer of stress makes the grieving process far more painful.

The truth is that early decisions ripple outward. Decisions made in the first days after a death shape the emotional experience that follows. When decisions are guided by clear instructions, families experience relief. They feel confident. They feel supported. They move through the tasks with a sense of purpose rather than fear. But when decisions are made blindly, the emotional consequences continue long after the paperwork is signed. People second-guess themselves. They feel guilt for choices made under pressure. These feelings become part of the narrative of the loss. For many, regret becomes a quiet companion during grief. They remember the moment they made a guess. They wonder if they chose correctly. The regret does not always heal. It often just grows quieter and sits beneath the surface, shaping the way the loss is remembered. Grief alone is already heavy. When regret is added to grief, the emotional weight becomes far harder to carry.

In most families, certain people are expected to take charge during a crisis. It may be the oldest sibling. It may be the spouse. It may be the person who has always been seen as responsible or organized. When a death occurs, that person is often thrust into the role of decision-maker whether they feel ready or not. When clarity is missing, the burden becomes enormous. They must interpret the wishes of the person who died. They must balance emotional needs. They must make decisions quickly. They must communicate with relatives who disagree. They must absorb the emotional reactions of others. They must manage practical tasks while navigating their own grief.

This role can leave a lasting emotional imprint. People describe feeling guilty for choices they made. They describe feeling responsible for outcomes they did not control. They describe feeling overwhelmed by pressure that arrived without warning. They describe feeling isolated even when surrounded by family. Clarity in planning does not remove the role, but it removes the strain attached to it. It allows the designated person to follow instructions rather than carry the weight of interpretation. It transforms responsibility into guidance.

This is also why confusion delays healing. Healing requires space. Healing requires time. Healing requires emotional capacity. When confusion dominates the early stages of grief, emotional energy gets diverted. Instead of processing loss, the mind becomes preoccupied with tasks and questions. Instead of reflecting, the heart becomes weighed down by decisions. Instead of sitting with emotion, people must navigate logistics. Many describe feeling stuck, as if their grief is suspended. They feel unable to move forward, because their energy is tied up in the administrative storm rather than in the natural processes of mourning.

Clarity allows healing to begin sooner. When tasks are simplified and decisions are already made, families are free to focus on connection and remembrance. They are not pulled into crisis mode. They are not drained by disagreements. They are not exhausted by confusion. Healing begins where confusion ends.

Preparation prevents complicated grief by removing unnecessary strain. It provides direction when direction is needed. It allows families to act with confidence rather than fear. It eliminates the burden of guessing. It reduces the possibility of conflict. It shortens the duration of logistical overwhelm. It gives grieving people the mental space required to process emotion. Preparation also honors the emotional experience of the family. It recognizes they will already be suffering. It acknowledges grief alone is difficult enough. It expresses compassion by reducing the stress that could otherwise intensify pain.

That is why planning matters. It is not only practical. It is emotional. It is a way of protecting the people you love from the hidden stress that compounds grief. It is a way of ensuring your family experiences clarity rather than confusion. It is a way of choosing peace for the people who will one day mourn you.

Clarity is one of the greatest gifts a person can give. It brings comfort to the people who remain. It provides answers when questions feel overwhelming. It creates stability in a moment defined by loss. It grounds a family when emotions run high. It reduces fear and anxiety. It allows grief to feel natural rather than chaotic. Clarity does not remove pain, but it transforms the experience of pain. It turns confusion into understanding. It turns conflict into cooperation. It turns regret into relief. It turns emotional weight into emotional support.

Clarity is not simply information. It is love in its most practical form. It is protection. It is compassion. It is a final act of care that radiates through the lives of the people you love.

The purpose of this chapter is to reveal the hidden forces that make grief more painful than it needs to be. Confusion is one of those forces. Without preparation, confusion grows. With preparation, confusion dissolves. What remains is grief itself, which is a natural and necessary part of the human experience. The next chapter will explore the psychological roots of avoidance, and why so many people postpone the conversations that could bring their families peace. Understanding avoidance matters, because avoidance is often the barrier that prevents people from creating clarity.

Chapter 4

The Psychology of Avoidance

Avoidance is one of the most common human responses to discomfort. When something creates fear or anxiety, the mind naturally tries to push it aside. Death may be the greatest example of this. It represents finality. It represents loss. It represents the unknown. It represents the end of everything we understand about our own existence.

The human mind instinctively protects itself from emotional pain, and one of the ways it does that is by creating distance from whatever feels threatening. Death is not simply an uncomfortable topic; it challenges the way we think about safety and control. It disrupts how we see our place in the world. It reminds us that nothing is permanent, and that is a frightening truth to sit with for too long.

So we turn away. We distract ourselves. We fill our days. We focus on tasks and goals. We build routines that give us the illusion of predictability. It is easier to plan a vacation than to plan for the end of life. It is easier to write a to-do list than a will. People avoid the subject not because they lack understanding, but because facing it requires emotional courage. In that sense, avoidance is natural. But it has consequences.

The mind is skilled at protecting itself. When a topic creates anxiety, the mind minimizes it. It pushes it into the background. It rationalizes the avoidance until the avoidance feels reasonable. People tell themselves they are too young to think about death.

They tell themselves they are healthy. They tell themselves they will get to it later. They tell themselves their family will know what to do. They tell themselves that if they ignore the subject long enough, it will feel less threatening. These thoughts are forms of self-preservation. They are meant to reduce discomfort in the moment, but they do not eliminate the reality of death. They only create a temporary sense of relief.

Over time, avoidance becomes a strategy. People push the subject away repeatedly until it becomes a habit. They stop thinking about it. They stop talking about it. They push the responsibility into the future and trust that somehow it will be easier later. It rarely becomes easier. Avoidance grows stronger with time, and the anxiety attached to the subject grows with it, because what we refuse to face does not shrink. It waits.

One of the strongest forces behind avoidance is the illusion of time. People believe there is always more time to plan. More time to have the conversation. More time to gather the documents. More time to get around to it. They imagine the moment will reveal itself when planning becomes necessary. They believe they will know when the "right time" arrives.

The illusion of time is comforting. It lets people postpone difficult decisions while still feeling responsible. It creates a sense of control, as if planning can be scheduled the way everything else in life is scheduled. Yet time does not always announce when it is running out. Sometimes it shortens unexpectedly. People rarely regret planning early. They often regret planning late. The illusion of time is one of the main reasons people avoid creating clarity, because they imagine a future version of themselves who will be more ready and more willing. But that future version never arrives if the pattern of avoidance remains unchecked.

Avoidance is not only psychological; it is cultural. In much of the modern world, death is not discussed openly. Conversations about it are often seen as dark or inappropriate. People worry they will upset someone. They do not want to be perceived as negative or morbid. They do not want to be judged. As a result, conversations that could bring clarity never begin.

Families often carry unspoken agreements to avoid the topic. Adult children hesitate to bring up planning with their parents. Parents hesitate to bring it up with their children. Siblings avoid it to keep the peace. Friends avoid it out of respect. The silence becomes a form of politeness. Yet that politeness builds a wall between family members and the clarity they will ultimately need. Cultural silence allows avoidance to thrive. It normalizes the idea that death should not be discussed. It teaches people to handle grief reactively rather than proactively. It reinforces the belief that planning is unusual rather than natural and loving.

Another reason people avoid conversations about death is a fear of burdening the people they love. Parents worry that discussing death will frighten their children. Adult children worry that discussing death with aging parents will send the wrong message. Partners worry it will create tension. Friends worry asking questions will feel intrusive. Silence can feel protective. Avoidance can feel like kindness.

But silence does not protect loved ones. It burdens them. It leaves them unprepared for decisions they will one day have to make. It places responsibility on them without guidance and pressure on them without information. The fear of burdening others is understandable, but preparation is not a burden. It is a gift. Clarity reduces stress. It removes pressure. It makes the emotional experience easier rather than harder. People often discover too late that the real burden was the silence.

Avoidance is also fueled by a fear of losing control. Human beings hold tightly to the belief that they control their lives. They choose where to live. They choose whom to love. They choose what to pursue. They choose how to spend their days. That sense of control gives life stability. It makes the world feel safe.

Death interrupts that sense of control. It reminds people that life is fragile and unpredictable. Thinking about death forces people to confront truths that undermine the illusion that they are fully in charge. Planning for death can feel like admitting that control is limited, and because of that, many people avoid the subject entirely. They believe that by not planning, they can postpone the discomfort that comes with acknowledging life's fragility.

Yet a different kind of control emerges when someone chooses to prepare. People cannot control when death comes, but they can control the clarity they leave behind. They can control the emotional experience of their loved ones. They can influence whether their family faces chaos or peace. Preparation becomes its own form of empowerment. Avoidance creates a false sense of control. Preparation creates a genuine one.

Reflecting on mortality can feel unsettling. It challenges the idea that life is endless. It forces people to consider that time is finite. Many people avoid this thought because it brings discomfort, so they turn back to routines and responsibilities. They choose distraction over reflection.

But discomfort can be meaningful. Discomfort can lead to clarity. Discomfort can inspire action. People who confront mortality often discover a greater sense of purpose. They prioritize what matters. They deepen relationships. They build meaning. Planning for the end of life does not diminish life. It often enhances it. Avoidance robs people of that insight. It keeps them in quiet denial. It prevents them from making thoughtful choices that would protect their families. Facing mortality is not an act of surrender; it is an act of awareness.

For some, avoidance is also reinforced by a subtle superstition: the belief that planning invites death. Many people carry a subconscious fear that documenting wishes, discussing funeral preferences, or preparing legal documents will somehow bring misfortune. The belief may not be logical, but it is powerful. It shapes behavior without people fully realizing it. It is similar to the fear of talking about illness, as if naming a possibility makes it more real.

In truth, planning does not influence fate. It prepares for the moment that will eventually come regardless of whether preparations exist. People who move through this superstition often describe a surprising relief. They realize the fear was not the result of planning, but the result of uncertainty. When uncertainty is removed, fear weakens. Planning does not bring death closer. It brings peace closer.

Avoidance is not a static behavior. It grows. When someone avoids a difficult topic once, it becomes easier to avoid it again. Over time, avoidance becomes routine. The longer someone postpones planning, the more intimidating it becomes. The more intimidating it becomes, the more they avoid it. Years can pass, and the subject remains untouched. Then a crisis occurs, and the person wishes they had faced it earlier. They realize the avoidance did not protect them. It only postponed responsibility. They realize the discomfort of planning would have been far easier than the stress their family now faces. Avoidance expands silently. It builds walls around conversations that should have happened long before. It delays clarity. It delays peace. Breaking the pattern requires intention. It requires someone to make the first move.

When someone finally does, something remarkable often happens. The fear begins to dissolve. The subject loses its intensity. The emotional weight becomes lighter. People describe feeling calmer. They feel more organized. They feel more in control. They feel more aware of what matters. The relief comes from clarity and from the realization that preparation is not nearly as overwhelming as imagination made it seem. Planning brings stability rather than fear. Families who begin these conversations often report feeling closer. The conversations create trust. They create openness. They create connection. Breaking avoidance does not weaken relationships. It strengthens them. It transforms discomfort into meaning.

Avoidance is powerful, but awareness is more powerful. When people understand why they avoid the subject of death, they can begin to change their relationship with it. They can approach planning with intention rather than fear. They can choose preparation over denial. They can replace uncertainty with clarity.

Awareness begins with honesty. It begins with recognizing that ignoring death does not protect anyone. It begins with acknowledging that silence creates confusion, and confusion creates emotional strain for the people we love. It begins with choosing a different path. This chapter exists to illuminate the unseen forces that shape avoidance. It explains why planning is delayed and why conversations never begin. It shows that avoidance is natural yet harmful. It reveals that the discomfort of facing death is temporary, while the suffering caused by an unprepared death can last for years.

The next chapter will explore the burden families carry when there is no plan. It will reveal the emotional and practical consequences of silence and provide a deeper understanding of why preparation matters. Understanding that burden is essential, because it highlights the real cost of avoidance. This knowledge is not meant to create fear. It is meant to inspire action. It is meant to empower people to choose clarity. It is meant to guide them toward peace.

Chapter 5

THE BURDEN FAMILIES CARRY WHEN THERE IS NO PLAN

When a person dies without a plan, the family is thrust into a world of responsibility they did not anticipate. These responsibilities do not wait for grief to settle. They arrive immediately and force themselves into the center of an already overwhelming moment. Decisions about the body have to be made. A funeral home has to be contacted. A service has to be arranged. Choices have to be made about who should be present and what should occur.

These decisions are never simple. They carry emotional meaning. They speak to identity, culture, faith, and personal preference. Without guidance, the family has to guess. Guessing becomes a source of stress, because every decision feels like a test. People fear making the wrong choice. They fear dishonoring the person who died. They fear doing something that would have gone against their wishes. That fear becomes the first of many burdens the family will carry.

What makes the burden heavier is that the decisions are often urgent. Funeral arrangements may need to be made within days, sometimes within hours. Time pressure amplifies emotional strain. The family has barely begun to process the loss, yet they must make choices that feel permanent. They must compare options. They must coordinate relatives. They must determine what is affordable. They must make decisions that will shape how the loved one is remembered. Without a plan, every step requires discussion and debate. Opinions differ. Emotions rise. People feel rushed, overwhelmed, and unprepared. There is no space for reflection. The urgency forces families into action while they are still in shock, and that pressure often stays with them long after the arrangements are complete.

Then comes the financial reality. Funerals and end-of-life costs can be significant, and when someone dies without a plan or without financial preparation, the burden often falls unexpectedly on the family. They must figure out how to pay for services while balancing emotion and affordability. Without clear instructions, families may choose options they cannot comfortably manage simply because they believe the loved one would have wanted something more elaborate. Financial stress adds another layer to emotional stress. People feel guilty if they cannot afford certain choices. They feel conflicted about cost. They may take on debt during a time of vulnerability. These decisions would be far easier if the person had expressed preferences or prepared financially. Without guidance, families must navigate this emotional and financial terrain alone.

At the same time, the search for information begins. When someone dies without a plan, families look for documents that may or may not exist. They open drawers. They go through closets. They search old boxes. They examine file folders. They attempt to access digital accounts. They try to make sense of bills, statements, and policies. This search is not only time-consuming; it is emotionally draining. Every photograph found brings a wave of grief. Every forgotten item becomes a reminder of the person who is gone. Every unknown password becomes a barrier that extends the pain. Families may spend weeks or months trying to piece together information that could have been organized in minutes if the person had prepared. The search becomes its own burden. It delays healing. It prolongs stress. It creates frustration and exhaustion at a time when emotional energy is already depleted.

Because there is no plan, each family member often carries their own interpretation of what the loved one would have wanted. Those interpretations come from memories, assumptions, and emotional needs. In grief, these interpretations feel deeply personal. They feel sacred. They feel symbolic. This makes disagreement more likely, and more intense. One person may believe a parent wanted a traditional funeral because of something said years ago. Another may believe they would have preferred something simple. One sibling may remember a conversation suggesting cremation. Another may remember something entirely different. None of these memories are wrong, but none of them provide certainty.

Conflicting interpretations create tension. Tension becomes disagreement. Disagreement becomes conflict. Conflict becomes emotional wounds that extend far beyond the moment. Many families experience strained relationships after a death when clarity is absent, and those fractures can last for years. Without a plan, the emotional landscape becomes complicated. Loving relationships become tangled with stress. That complication becomes one of the heaviest burdens a family carries.

Beyond the funeral decisions, families can also face the weight of legal uncertainty. When a person dies without clear legal documents, the family must navigate a confusing landscape of laws and procedures. They must determine whether a will exists. They must figure out how assets are transferred. They must understand probate rules. They must identify who has legal authority to make decisions. These questions do not arrive gradually. They appear all at once and demand answers.

Without guidance, families may feel powerless. They may search online and find conflicting advice. They may contact lawyers and feel overwhelmed by complexity. They may not know which documents are needed or where to locate them.

Legal uncertainty becomes a heavy burden because it prolongs the administrative process, increases stress, and delays closure. Families often feel they are moving through unfamiliar territory with no map. They fear making mistakes. They fear leaving something undone. They fear creating problems that could have been avoided. A clear plan eliminates many of these fears. Without one, the burden falls entirely on those left behind.

In modern life, this burden extends into the digital world. A person's life is no longer contained in physical belongings. There are online accounts. Social media profiles. Email addresses. Financial accounts that require digital access. Subscriptions and services connected to identity. When no plan exists, families guess usernames and passwords. They contact companies one by one. They hit security barriers designed to protect privacy, but which now complicate the family's responsibility. This process can be exhausting. It can take months, sometimes years. Many families eventually abandon the effort because it becomes too overwhelming. Yet unresolved digital accounts can create legal issues, financial issues, and emotional strain. Social media pages may remain active. Subscriptions may continue. Important information may remain inaccessible. A clear digital plan removes this burden. Without it, the family steps into a maze.

All of this creates emotional exhaustion. Grief itself drains energy and attention. It makes simple tasks feel heavy. When someone dies without a plan, grief is multiplied by a long list of responsibilities. Families must manage tasks while trying to process loss, and this dual existence takes a toll. People often describe feeling as though they are living two lives at once: One life is grieving. The other is managing paperwork and decisions. They long for time to mourn, yet the responsibilities keep coming. Forms need to be completed. Calls need to be made. Accounts need to be closed. Each new task feels like an intrusion into private emotional space.

This exhaustion can slow healing. It can cause people to shut down emotionally. It can create distance within families. It can make the loss feel heavier than it already is. The absence of a plan extends the administrative burden, which extends the emotional burden. After the dust settles, many families look back with lingering regret.

They wish they had known more. They wish the person had provided guidance. They wish conversations had taken place while the opportunity still existed. People remember the arguments. They remember uncertainty. They remember decisions made without confidence. They remember stress that overshadowed grief. That regret can follow them for years, becoming part of the emotional memory of the loss. Regret is one of the heaviest burdens a family can carry, and it is often born not from the death itself, but from the absence of clarity. A plan removes the source of that regret. Without one, families are left to navigate emotions that could have been avoided.

Sometimes, the experience leaves behind a silence that remains. When there is no plan, families often avoid talking about what happened. They do not discuss the stress because it feels too painful. They do not speak about confusion because it may reopen conflict. They do not address regret because it feels too raw. The silence remains because the experience is too difficult to revisit. But this silence is not peaceful. It is unresolved. It is heavy. It lingers in the background of family dynamics long after the loss, shaping relationships in ways people do not always name.

This is why preparation is an act of love. Preparation removes every burden described in this chapter. It prevents confusion that leads to conflict. It reduces financial stress that deepens grief. It prevents a prolonged search for documents. It removes uncertainty that fuels anxiety. It reduces regret. It softens the silence that can follow an overwhelming experience. Preparation is more than organization; it is a decision to protect the people you care about from avoidable suffering. It is a gift of peace. It is a way of ensuring that the people who love you will not have to navigate chaos in the midst of grief.

A plan provides direction. It provides comfort. It provides clarity. It transforms what could be an overwhelming experience into one that is manageable. It reduces emotional weight and creates space for healing. The next chapter will explore how clarity strengthens families. It will examine the emotional benefits of preparation and the ways thoughtful planning can create deeper bonds. Chaos causes confusion. Clarity creates connection. Clarity is not only practical; it is deeply human. It is an expression of care that continues long after a person is gone.

Chapter 6

HOW CLARITY STRENGTHENS FAMILIES

When families face loss, they instinctively look for something steady to hold on to. They need direction. They need assurance. They need a sense of grounding in a moment that can feel as if the earth has shifted beneath them. Clarity provides that stability. It becomes a quiet anchor, a steady point in the storm, and in many cases, it acts as a kind of emotional protection.

When someone prepares their wishes, they remove the guesswork that would otherwise fall on the people they love. They reduce the emotional noise. They reduce the anxiety that uncertainty brings. They soften the edges of grief. The pain of loss remains, because love does not disappear simply because logistics are handled well, but the family is spared the chaos that so often intensifies sorrow. In that way, clarity allows grief to unfold naturally, without being tangled in fear, confusion, and second-guessing.

Families often struggle during loss not because of grief itself, but because they hold different interpretations of what should happen next. Without clear direction, each person feels responsible for honoring the loved one in their own way. When interpretations differ, conflict can emerge, and that conflict is painful because it feels tied to loyalty and love. People are not arguing about details. They are arguing about meaning. They are arguing about respect. They are arguing about doing right by someone who is no longer there to speak for themselves.

Clarity removes that tension. When wishes are known, no one needs to interpret. No one needs to argue. No one needs to fight for what they believe is right. The direction becomes shared truth. The family can move together in unity rather than working against one another from a place of uncertainty. Shared understanding is one of the quiet forces that strengthens families. It creates alignment during a time when alignment can feel impossible, and it brings people closer rather than pulling them apart.

It also does something very practical: It reduces stress. Reducing stress changes the way a family relates to one another in grief. Stress narrows emotional availability. When someone is overwhelmed, they cannot fully show up for the people around them. They may become irritable or withdrawn. They may react strongly to small things. They may struggle to communicate with kindness. This is normal. Stress pushes people into survival mode.

But when clear instructions exist, the family is not forced into crisis management. They are not thrust into high-stakes decisions with no map. They are not pulled into uncertainty. As a result, there is more emotional space to support one another. Siblings can comfort each other instead of debating what is "right." Spouses can grieve together instead of dividing roles into "the one falling apart" and "the one holding it together." Children can feel supported rather than overwhelmed. Clarity creates room, and emotional room is exactly what families need most.

Loss can make people feel disoriented. Many describe feeling unmoored. The world feels unfamiliar. Ordinary tasks feel strange. In that haze, guidance becomes invaluable. When a loved one has left clear direction, the family can feel as if the person is still gently leading them. The plan becomes a steady voice that says keep going. You do not have to guess. You do not have to carry this alone. That sense of being guided brings comfort. It creates continuity rather than abrupt emotional rupture. It offers a calm that can feel unreachable in the early days of grief, and it gives families quiet confidence in the choices they must make.

Clarity can also protect something deeply important to families: traditions. Every family has them, whether they are cultural, spiritual, or personal. When clarity is missing, families may struggle to determine which traditions to honor, and that uncertainty adds yet another layer of stress. People worry about choosing incorrectly. They worry about letting go of something meaningful. They worry they will regret what they did or did not include.

When wishes are clearly documented, families understand what mattered. They know what should be preserved. They know what should be included. They know what should be avoided. Traditions can continue naturally, and the family can honor shared history with confidence rather than frustration. Traditions help families feel rooted, and clarity protects those roots.

In many families, clear direction also creates emotional relief, and that relief becomes a form of strength. Grief is heavy. When responsibilities and uncertainty are reduced, the emotional weight becomes more manageable. Families who have clear direction often describe an unexpected sense of gratitude in the midst of pain. They feel grateful that decisions are already made. They feel comfort knowing they are honoring their loved one accurately. They feel supported by the guidance that was left for them. That relief changes the emotional tone of the days following a loss. It creates space for presence and connection. It allows families to focus on memories and relationships rather than tasks and uncertainty. Relief becomes strength, and strength carries people through moments they never imagined they would survive.

This is the power of unity during loss. Loss is when families need one another most, yet without clarity they can become divided. People interpret silence differently. They interpret memories differently. They interpret responsibilities differently. These differences are usually well-intentioned, but they can weaken unity at the exact moment unity is needed. Clarity creates the opposite effect. It provides a single path for the family to follow. It becomes common ground. Instead of debating, the family moves together. Instead of questioning one another, they support one another. Instead of feeling uncertain, they feel guided. Unity does not erase grief, but it makes grief less isolating. It reminds people that they are not alone in the hardest moment of their lives.

When the plan is known, communication changes too. Conversations become easier. Family members can speak openly without the underlying fear of disagreement. They can express feelings without the weight of decision-making. They can share stories. They can remember together. They can comfort one another without being pulled back into logistics. Healthy communication is essential during grief. It prevents misunderstandings. It reduces resentment. It helps families process emotions more naturally. Clarity encourages this communication by removing tension that often sits beneath conversations about death. When communication is healthy, families grow stronger through the experience. They learn to rely on one another. They learn to listen more deeply. They learn that grief can be shared rather than carried alone.

Clarity also transforms difficult moments into meaningful ones. When families know exactly what to do, they can move through hard tasks with intention. The funeral becomes more meaningful because it reflects the wishes of the person who died. Decisions become symbolic acts of respect rather than desperate attempts to guess correctly. The moment becomes about honoring a life rather than managing a crisis. Later, families often remember these experiences differently. Instead of recalling chaos, they recall moments of connection and meaning. Clarity changes the emotional landscape. It turns fear into steady confidence. It turns confusion into purpose. It turns sorrow into remembrance.

The impact of wise preparation does not fade after the funeral. It becomes part of the family's emotional memory. They remember that someone cared enough to protect them from avoidable stress. They remember the peace that clarity brought. They remember the unity it created. This becomes part of the legacy of the person who prepared. Preparation becomes a final act of love, shaping not only what happens after death, but how the family remembers the one who is gone. Families often say clarity changed everything. It allowed them to grieve with dignity rather than distress. It allowed them to stay connected rather than divided. It allowed them to feel supported rather than overwhelmed.

The purpose of clarity is not only to provide guidance after death. Clarity strengthens families in the present. It encourages conversations that build trust. It brings people closer through honesty. It creates understanding. It fosters connection. It teaches the value of preparation in all aspects of life. Clarity becomes a model for future generations. It becomes part of a family's cultural identity, showing that planning is not about fear. It is about protection.

The next chapter will explore the emotional and relational benefits of proactive planning, and how preparation can create peace long before it is needed. Because clarity strengthens families not only during grief, but throughout their lives.

Chapter 7

THE PEACE THAT COMES FROM PLANNING AHEAD

Peace is often treated as something we search for after a crisis, something we hope will return once the hardest part is over. But when it comes to death, peace can begin long before loss. Planning ahead is frequently mistaken for a paperwork exercise. People picture forms and signatures. They imagine difficult decisions made in hushed tones. Yet the truth is that planning ahead shapes peace in the present. It brings emotional steadiness to the person doing the planning, and it brings stability to the people who will one day rely on that plan.

Peace begins the moment someone decides to take responsibility for their future. It begins when they choose clarity over avoidance. It begins when they recognize that preparation is not a morbid fixation but an act of love. The peace that comes from this choice is quiet yet powerful. It changes the way a person moves through life. It creates a sense of grounding that supports them long before anyone experiences loss.

Life is full of things that feel heavy until they are handled, and end-of-life planning is one of them. People often describe an unexpected sense of lightness once they create a plan. They feel relieved knowing the responsibility is no longer hanging over them. They feel calmer knowing they will not leave chaos behind. They feel clearer about their values and priorities. This emotional ease is meaningful because it frees the mind from worry. It removes the quiet mental burden that comes from postponing something important. It allows people to live more fully because they know they have taken care of what must eventually be faced. Emotional ease is a form of peace, and planning makes it possible.

Planning also invites self-awareness. It encourages reflection on identity. It asks people to consider beliefs, traditions, preferences, and the way they want to be remembered. That reflection builds clarity. It helps people feel anchored in their decisions. It often leads to a deeper appreciation for the life still being lived, because it sharpens what matters most. Many people feel more peaceful after planning not simply because tasks are complete, but because they understand themselves better. That emotional clarity becomes part of the peace preparation provides.

The impact does not stop with the person doing the planning. Peace extends to the people who will remain. Families who experience loss without guidance often describe the early days as chaotic. They feel overwhelmed by decisions. They feel uncertain about preferences. They feel pressured by time. They feel unsure about the choices they make. Uncertainty becomes its own form of pain, because grief is already heavy, and confusion makes it heavier.

When a plan exists, the experience changes. Families feel supported. They feel guided. They feel reassured. The burden of guessing disappears. The pressure of choosing disappears. They move through the process with confidence rather than confusion. Peace for the family is one of the greatest benefits of planning. It is the gift of stability during one of life's most destabilizing moments.

There is also peace that comes from financial readiness. Financial strain during grief can become a quiet form of suffering. Families may feel conflicted about cost. They may fear making the wrong choice. They may feel pressured to spend more than they can manage. That financial complexity can intensify emotional pain and create guilt at the very moment people are least equipped to carry it.

Planning ahead can remove much of that strain. When someone prepares financially, or secures a final expense policy, their family is protected from unexpected costs. They can focus on honoring their loved one rather than worrying about affordability. Financial clarity becomes emotional clarity. In this sense, financial peace is emotional peace, and preparation creates both.

Planning also creates peace by reducing conflict. One of the most painful aspects of an unplanned death is the disagreement that can follow. Family members may have different memories or interpretations. Those differences can turn into tension that lasts far beyond the funeral. Clarity prevents this. When wishes are known, the family does not debate. They follow the plan. They support one another. They move together. Unity creates emotional peace because it removes the stress of conflict and allows people to focus on grieving rather than defending opinions. Peace thrives in the absence of conflict, and planning nurtures that peace.

Just as important is the peace that comes from emotional space. Grief demands room. When logistical responsibilities take over, that room disappears. Families become overwhelmed by tasks. They become exhausted. They feel as if they cannot even begin to mourn. A clear plan creates emotional space. It allows families to step out of crisis mode. It gives them time to sit together. It gives them moments of quiet. It gives them room to feel. That space becomes spiritual oxygen. It helps people move through the early days of grief with greater steadiness. Peace becomes possible when there is room to experience it.

Planning often leads to another form of peace: the peace of knowing nothing was left unsaid. Preparation tends to open the door to meaningful conversations. Families sit together and talk about wishes, preferences, values, and beliefs. These conversations strengthen relationships. They bring honesty. They bring understanding. They create connection. People often describe feeling grateful they had these conversations before losing someone. They carry comfort in knowing important words were spoken while there was still time. Peace grows from communication, and planning makes communication easier.

When wishes are known, the goodbye itself can feel more meaningful. The farewell becomes authentic. It reflects the personality, spirit, and values of the person who died. This creates peace for the family because they know they honored the person truthfully. A meaningful goodbye supports healing. It gives families a memory they can look back on with pride and comfort. It becomes something warm rather than something shadowed by regret. Peace is found in goodbyes that honor the life that was lived.

For families who move through a planned farewell, peace often continues after the service is over. They know they followed the wishes that were left. They know they avoided conflict. They know they were supported by clarity. That peace becomes part of the emotional memory of the loss. It becomes part of the family's story. It becomes part of the legacy of the person who prepared. Peace that continues is one of the most profound outcomes of planning ahead, because it does not simply help in the moment. It changes what the family carries afterward.

Preparation, then, is not only about what happens after death. It influences how people live. It encourages openness, responsibility, confidence, and connection. It helps families communicate more honestly. It helps people reflect on their values. It helps them appreciate life with deeper awareness. In that way, preparation becomes a lifelong form of peace. It shapes the experience of living as much as it shapes the experience of grieving. It becomes part of family culture. It becomes part of an emotional foundation passed down through generations.

Planning ahead creates peace in every direction. It creates peace for today. It creates peace for tomorrow. It creates peace for the people who will one day carry your memory.

Chapter 8

PROACTIVE PLANNING AS A LIVING PRACTICE

Proactive planning is not a single moment. It is not a box you check once and forget. It is a living practice, one that grows and changes as life changes. Families move. Relationships shift. Beliefs deepen. New traditions emerge. Preferences evolve. A plan that once felt complete can become outdated simply because the person behind it has changed. Proactive planning acknowledges what life teaches again and again: Nothing stays still, and preparation cannot be rigid when life itself is fluid.

That is why planning works best when it becomes an ongoing conversation. When families treat it as something natural, something woven into the way they care for one another, they stay connected. They revisit the subject as life unfolds. They speak openly about wishes and values. They share updates. They ask questions. Over time, that steady communication builds trust and transparency. It replaces mystery with understanding. It replaces fear with familiarity. Proactive planning becomes a living practice when it is not treated as a grim event, but as a normal part of love.

One of the reasons people avoid planning is that they imagine it requires dramatic action. They picture long forms and overwhelming decisions. They assume it has to be done all at once. In reality, proactive planning is built through small steps over time. Recording a preference. Updating a document. Organizing a few important items. Checking in with loved ones. These actions may seem minor, but they accumulate, and over time they create a strong foundation.

Small steps matter because they reduce fear. They make planning approachable. They allow the process to feel like progress rather than pressure. When someone takes even a small action, they experience accomplishment. They feel more capable. They feel more confident taking the next step. This is how a complete plan is built, not through one overwhelming effort, but through consistent attention. The power of proactive planning is not intensity. It is continuity.

Proactive planning is often framed as something we do for others, and it is. But it is also a powerful expression of self-respect. When someone organizes their life and clarifies their wishes, they honor their own voice. They affirm their right to shape the story of their life and the legacy they leave. They refuse to let their most meaningful decisions be made in a moment of crisis by someone else, under pressure, with incomplete information.

That act of self-respect brings emotional confidence. People feel more grounded in their decisions. They feel more aligned with what matters to them. They feel a deeper sense of dignity because they have taken the time to express their preferences with intention. Self-respect grows when a person takes responsibility for their own narrative, and planning is one of the clearest ways to do that.

This is how planning becomes cultural inside a family. Families inherit patterns without realizing it. They inherit communication styles. They inherit unspoken rules. They inherit traditions and approaches to difficult topics. Proactive planning can introduce a new pattern: honesty, preparedness, openness. When one person begins to plan thoughtfully, it often inspires others. Children learn from parents. Parents learn from their children. Siblings influence one another. Conversations that once felt uncomfortable become normal. Planning becomes part of the family's shared values.

A culture of preparedness brings stability. It reduces fear. It models responsibility for future generations. This changes the emotional tone of family life, because difficult topics are no longer treated as forbidden territory. They become part of what families can handle together.

Proactive planning also strengthens relationships by encouraging shared responsibility. Instead of one person carrying the entire emotional and administrative burden, the family becomes involved. They understand one another's preferences. They know where documents are stored. They know who will take on certain roles if the time comes. This shared preparation builds teamwork. It promotes empathy. It reduces pressure. Families feel supported because they are not alone. They are working together toward clarity and peace. Shared preparation brings people closer because it is built on mutual care.

Of course, planning only stays meaningful if it stays current. Life never stays the same. People change careers. They move to new cities. They develop new beliefs. They grow in unexpected ways. A plan created years ago may no longer reflect someone's values or desires. Preferences about legacy, spirituality, medical choices, or even the kind of farewell someone wants can shift as a person matures.

When planning is revisited regularly, it stays true to the person's evolving identity. That adaptability brings peace because the plan always feels authentic. It reflects the life being lived now, not a version of life that no longer exists. Families feel reassured knowing the plan was thoughtfully updated rather than abandoned in an earlier chapter. Adaptability ensures authenticity, and authenticity strengthens the value of any plan.

There is another benefit that people rarely expect: Proactive planning can become a source of emotional strength. Facing mortality requires courage. Making decisions requires clarity. Pursuing organization requires discipline. People who engage in proactive planning often discover resilience they did not know they had. That strength does not stay contained within the planning process. It influences how people approach health, relationships, and personal goals. It deepens appreciation for time. It encourages more honest communication. It helps people live with greater alignment. Planning for the future strengthens how a person lives in the present.

It also reduces anxiety in a very direct way. Many people carry quiet worry about leaving things unfinished. They worry about disorganization. They worry about burdening their families. They worry about unresolved matters that might create confusion for others. These worries sit in the background of daily life, like static that never fully turns off.

Organization dissolves that static. When documents are gathered and wishes are documented, the mental weight begins to lift. People feel lighter. They feel more peaceful. They feel more in control. Organization creates emotional clarity. It turns fear into confidence and worry into relief. The simple act of creating order can bring profound peace of mind.

Once one person begins, the impact often spreads. Proactive planning has a ripple effect. Friends notice the calm confidence. They hear about the relief. They witness the benefits. They begin asking questions. They begin thinking about their own plans. Communities grow healthier when proactive planning becomes more common. Conversations open. Stigma fades. Preparation becomes normalized. People learn from one another. The ripple effect transforms how groups approach end-of-life responsibility, and in doing so it creates peace for families far beyond the first person who chose to plan.

This is why proactive planning becomes part of a legacy of responsibility. A legacy is not only made of memories or belongings. It is made of actions. It is made of how someone chooses to care for others. Proactive planning shows responsibility that lives on long after a person is gone. Families remember the clarity they were given. They remember the peace they felt. They remember the weight that was lifted from their shoulders. That example shapes future generations. Children who see their parents plan take planning seriously. Grandchildren inherit a culture of preparedness. Responsibility becomes part of family identity.

At its core, proactive planning is a living expression of love. It says, "I want to protect you. I want your grief to be less painful. I want to remove confusion before it ever reaches you. I care enough to think beyond my lifetime." When planning becomes a living practice, it reflects love in action, not just in sentiment. It creates peace in the present. It creates peace in the future. It creates peace that lasts beyond memory.

The next chapter will explore legacy in a deeper way. It will examine how preparation allows people to shape the meaning they leave behind, and how thoughtful planning can turn legacy into something lasting and deeply personal. Proactive planning is not only practical; it is profoundly human.

Chapter 9

LEGACY AS A LIVING GIFT

Most people think of legacy as something that begins after death. They imagine it as a story told about them once they are gone. They picture photographs in albums and memories shared at gatherings. They think of legacy as fixed, as if it arrives all at once and cannot be shaped. But legacy begins long before that moment. It begins in the choices we make now. It begins in the values we practice. It begins in the way we live.

Legacy is not simply what we leave behind. It is what we build while we are here. It is the meaning we create, the care we show, and the clarity we offer to the people who trust us. When we prepare thoughtfully, we are not just organizing details. We are shaping a legacy that will support others for years to come. Preparation becomes part of the story we tell about who we are, not through words but through action.

Every day, people contribute to their legacy without realizing it. They make decisions that reveal character. They choose how to treat others. They show patience. They show strength. They share wisdom. They teach lessons through small examples that never look dramatic in the moment, but become unforgettable later. These daily actions shape how a person will be remembered. Planning ahead extends this same practice. It communicates values through clarity. It communicates love through organization. It communicates respect through preparation. The choices someone makes now become part of the emotional memory their family will hold forever. Legacy is built through small moments, and planning makes those moments intentional.

When someone leaves behind clear wishes, their family feels guided. They feel supported, as if the person is still offering direction. That guidance becomes part of the emotional legacy. It becomes a reminder of thoughtfulness. It becomes comfort during a time when comfort is hard to find. Legacy is not only about what a person accomplished. It is also about how they made others feel. When someone leaves behind clarity, their family feels cared for. They feel protected. They feel less alone.

This kind of guidance shapes grief in powerful ways. It helps people heal because it removes the burden of guessing. It gives them confidence in the decisions they must make. It reassures them that they honored their loved one with accuracy and respect. Guidance is a legacy that continues to speak long after a person is gone, because it continues to steady the people who remain.

Legacy also lives in stories and wisdom. Stories hold the emotional history of families. They capture laughter, lessons learned, resilience, and the personality of the people who came before us. When someone takes the time to record their stories or reflections, they create a legacy that can live for generations. Many people underestimate the value of their own stories. They think they are ordinary. They think they are unimportant. But stories carry wisdom, humor, truth, and identity. They help families understand where they came from and who they are.

Planning ahead can include documenting those stories, writing them down, recording them, and sharing them with intention. When that happens, stories become a gift that grows more valuable with time. They become anchors that help families feel connected across generations.

Legacy is not only emotional. It is also cultural. Values shape how families live. Beliefs shape how they treat one another. Traditions shape identity. When someone takes the time to express values clearly, the family gains a deeper understanding of meaning and purpose. For some, this includes spiritual beliefs. For others, it is cultural or personal principles: kindness, courage, integrity, responsibility, gratitude. These values become a guiding force. They influence decisions. They influence behavior. They influence the stories told about the person.

When planning becomes part of life, it reinforces those values. It signals responsibility. It signals care. It signals intention. That clarity becomes part of the legacy. Values outlive the person who held them when they are communicated clearly, and when they are modeled consistently.

One of the most powerful ways a person shapes legacy is through responsibility and preparedness. When someone prepares for the future, they send a clear message about who they are. They show that they think ahead. They show that they care about the well-being of others. They show that they understand the weight of responsibility and are willing to carry it.

Families remember this. They remember the clarity they were given. They remember how the person protected them from confusion. They remember the peace they felt during moments that could have been chaotic. Preparedness becomes a defining trait in the legacy, a story told with gratitude rather than regret. Responsibility is not a burden. It is a final expression of love.

Legacy is also shaped through thoughtful communication. When families engage in conversations about planning, relationships often deepen. The conversations can feel delicate, but they frequently lead to understanding that might never have arrived otherwise. People share beliefs they have never voiced. They reveal preferences that reflect identity. They communicate with a level of honesty that brings insight and intimacy.

Those conversations become part of the legacy too. Families remember them. They treasure them. They pass on the significance of those discussions. They speak of the clarity and the connection that came from them. Thoughtful communication becomes a legacy of closeness, strengthening the bond among the people who remain.

Proactive planning can also reduce burden for future generations. The burden of an unplanned death rarely ends with one generation. Families that experience confusion often repeat the same patterns. Silence continues. Avoidance continues. Lack of planning becomes normal. Children learn to avoid the topic because they watched adults avoid it. But proactive planning breaks that cycle. When one person chooses clarity, the pattern changes. Future generations inherit a new approach. They learn that preparation is an act of care. They learn that planning brings peace. They learn that responsibility is something to embrace rather than fear. This shift becomes a generational legacy, leaving families stronger and more prepared for the future.

Then there is the legacy of emotional stability during grief. Families will always remember how they felt during the days after a loved one's passing. They will remember whether those days were filled with confusion or guided by peace. They will carry the emotional imprint of that experience for the rest of their lives. Leaving behind emotional stability is one of the most profound legacies a person can offer, because it protects the family when they are at their most vulnerable.

A clear plan also strengthens identity. It helps families understand who the person was. It reflects values, preferences, beliefs, and personality. Whether someone wanted a joyful celebration or a quiet gathering, the plan becomes a reflection of their life. Families take comfort in that reflection. They feel connected through the clarity that was left behind. They feel grounded by the accuracy of the choices they made, and their memories deepen because they understand the person more clearly. Identity is one of the strongest elements of legacy, and planning preserves it.

Legacy, in other words, is not an accident. It is shaped intentionally through decisions that express care and purpose. Proactive planning is one of the clearest expressions of that intention. It says that my life mattered, and so does the emotional experience of the people I love. It says that my values are worth passing on. It says that my story continues through clarity and preparation. That intention becomes a living legacy. It influences how families think about responsibility. It influences how they handle their own planning. It influences the emotional landscape they pass to children and grandchildren. Intention echoes forward long after a person is gone.

This is why legacy can be a gift that continues to give. The most meaningful gifts are the ones that ease the burden of others, and a clear plan does exactly that. It removes uncertainty. It offers direction. It provides peace. It becomes a gift that continues to give in the most difficult moments a family will ever face.

Families often speak of this gift with deep gratitude. They describe it as one of the most compassionate things their loved one ever did. They remember the clarity. They remember the relief. They remember the steadiness it brought. That gratitude becomes part of the memory, part of the story, part of the legacy. A legacy is not defined by possessions. It is defined by meaning. Planning with care creates a legacy that continues to uplift others long after life has ended.

Legacy and planning are inseparable. Planning shapes the emotional experience of loss. Legacy shapes the meaning of a life. Together they form a complete expression of responsibility and love. Planning gives structure to the future. Legacy gives depth to the past. The two work together to strengthen families during moments of profound vulnerability. When people understand this connection, planning stops feeling like a task and starts feeling like purpose. It becomes something they choose because they understand the emotional and generational impact. It becomes part of the life they are living today.

Thinking about legacy can also become an invitation to live fully. When people reflect on what they want to leave behind, they often gain renewed appreciation for life. They recognize time is limited. They notice relationships that matter. They pay attention to the experiences that give life meaning. Planning becomes a reminder to live with intention, to love fully, to express gratitude, to speak honestly, to strengthen bonds. Legacy invites presence. It invites choices that reflect values. It invites memories worth holding. Planning does not diminish life. It magnifies it.

In the end, the deepest purpose of legacy is peace. Peace for the person who prepares. Peace for the family who remains. Peace for future generations who learn from the example. When someone plans thoughtfully, they offer a final gift: stability, comfort, emotional clarity. That gift becomes part of the family's story. It becomes a guiding light during grief. It becomes a reminder that love does not end. It continues through the clarity we leave behind.

The next chapter will explore how planning shapes not only families, but communities. It will examine the larger social impact of preparation and the ways clarity can influence how society views responsibility and care. Legacy begins with intention. Planning transforms that intention into peace.

Chapter 10

How Planning Shapes Communities

Communities do not form by accident. They emerge from the habits, attitudes, and choices of the people who make them up. When individuals take responsibility for their lives and their futures, the community becomes more stable. When people avoid difficult conversations, the community inherits that silence. When families plan thoughtfully, clarity begins to show up not only inside a household, but across an entire neighborhood, workplace, faith community, or social circle.

Planning is often viewed as a private matter, something that belongs behind closed doors. Yet it has a ripple effect. The more people who prepare, the more peace exists within a community. Families experience fewer conflicts. Neighbors encounter fewer emergencies that feel impossible to navigate. Friends witness acts of responsibility that quietly inspire their own. Planning shapes communities because it shapes people, and people shape everything around them.

When someone plans for the end of their life, their immediate family feels the benefits first, but the impact rarely stops there. Friends notice. Colleagues notice. People in social groups notice. They see the calm confidence that preparation creates. They see the clarity surrounding a family during a time that would normally produce chaos. They see emotional stability where they expected disorder. Even when no one names it directly, the contrast is visible, and visibility is influential.

That influence matters because it normalizes preparation. It breaks the silence. It reduces fear. It gives others permission to consider planning without feeling dramatic or morbid. One thoughtful act can influence dozens of people, not through persuasion but through example. In this way, planning spreads the way healthy habits spread: quietly, gradually, household to household.

Planning also reduces the emotional cost of crisis for everyone connected to a family. Communities often absorb the shock of unplanned death. Friends support grieving families. Colleagues step in at work. Neighbors bring meals, drive someone to appointments, or help with childcare. Social groups become lifelines in the middle of chaos. When planning is missing, the community often feels the weight of confusion and urgency. People help carry burdens that could have been avoided, and the support becomes frantic because the situation is frantic.

When a plan exists, the community still shows up, but the atmosphere changes. The family has direction. They have a structure to follow. They are not overwhelmed by endless decisions. Support becomes grounded rather than panicked. Compassion becomes the focus rather than crisis management. In that sense, planning protects not only a family, but an entire social network that would otherwise be pulled into the turbulence of uncertainty.

These patterns compound across generations. Generational habits become cultural habits. When parents plan thoughtfully, children learn to value preparedness. When children watch their parents avoid planning, they often inherit the same pattern. This is how communities develop unspoken rules about responsibility: what is discussed openly, what is handled privately, what is ignored until it becomes an emergency. Communities that value planning experience more stability because families pass down clarity rather than confusion. They build systems that support one another. They speak more openly about difficult topics. They learn from each generation instead of repeating the same avoidable pain.

Intergenerational stability influences everything. It shows up in schools, workplaces, and neighborhoods. It creates environments where preparation is normal and emotional resilience is strengthened over time. Planning becomes a cultural norm rather than an exception, and when that happens, communities become less fragile.

Planning also reduces fear at a broader level. Fear of death is one of the most common fears across cultures. It influences decisions and shapes behavior, especially when people avoid the topic and allow anxiety to grow quietly in the background. That fear affects communities because it limits openness and honesty. It makes conversations about aging, illness, and loss feel forbidden. It isolates people right when connection is needed most.

Planning reduces fear by bringing the subject into the light. It transforms something frightening into something manageable. As more people engage in planning, a community becomes more comfortable discussing what matters. That comfort changes the way people support one another. It strengthens social bonds. It can even improve mental health outcomes, because fear loses some of its power when it is no longer carried in silence. Communities become healthier when fear is not running the conversation from the shadows.

There is also a practical benefit that is easy to overlook: planning reduces pressure on community institutions. When families are unprepared, responsibility extends beyond the household. Hospitals face confusion about end-of-life wishes. Funeral homes must guide families through decisions they were not ready to make. Religious and cultural leaders may be asked to interpret preferences without clarity. Workplaces must navigate sudden disruptions. Legal offices receive urgent calls about documents that were never created. These institutions are already strained, and unpreparedness adds friction at the exact moment when families and professionals need smoother processes.

When individuals plan ahead, these systems function more effectively. Processes are clearer. Services are delivered with greater accuracy. People supporting the family can focus on care instead of confusion. Planning reduces pressure on the systems that hold communities together, which strengthens the community as a whole.

Planning also contributes to something deeper: a culture of compassion. Communities become compassionate when people consistently act with empathy, and planning ahead is an act of empathy. It recognizes that others will one day carry emotional and practical responsibilities. It respects the emotional experiences of the people who will remain. It demonstrates care in a deeply personal way. When a community has many examples of that kind of empathy, it shapes the community's character. People look out for one another. They encourage honest conversations. They support each other through life transitions. Compassion grows wherever thoughtful planning is valued.

As planning becomes more normal, conversations about life become healthier too. Communities often struggle to talk openly about aging, illness, and mortality because these subjects feel heavy and delicate. But when planning is normalized, people become less guarded. They feel more comfortable asking questions. They gain confidence discussing preferences. Friends share what they've learned. Neighbors trade advice. Families talk more honestly. Community groups organize workshops and resources. Planning opens the door to understanding rather than fear, and healthy conversations create a stronger social foundation.

This is the role of planning in community resilience. Communities that handle crisis well are communities that prepare before crisis arrives. That is true for natural disasters, public health, and financial stability; and it is also true for the emotional impact of death. When individuals plan ahead, there is less chaos, less conflict, and less confusion. People move through difficult moments with structure rather than panic. That collective steadiness protects the emotional well-being of the whole community, because fewer people are pushed into emergency mode at the same time. Planning strengthens the network of relationships that holds a community together.

It also grows shared knowledge and collective wisdom. When people engage in planning, they learn about legal documents, end-of-life preferences, medical directives, and financial readiness. Families share what they learn with friends. Friends pass it along. Organizations adopt tools and resources. Over time, knowledge spreads, and the community becomes more informed and more confident navigating these topics. Shared wisdom builds stronger communities because it reduces helplessness, and helplessness is one of the biggest drivers of panic.

Visible leadership accelerates this cultural shift. Communities are deeply influenced by examples. When leaders plan thoughtfully and speak openly about it, stigma fades. Leaders might be teachers, clergy, business owners, health-care workers, elders, parents, or anyone others look to for guidance. When those people model responsibility, others follow. Leadership by example transforms planning from a private task into a shared value.

Ultimately, planning becomes a path to social stability. Communities thrive when people act with intention, when responsibilities are shared, and when communication is open.

Planning supports all of these qualities. It reduces the emotional turmoil that spills into relationships. It creates clarity that prevents conflict. It encourages dialogue that deepens trust. Social stability grows when preparation becomes understood as normal, compassionate, and wise. It creates calmer households. It strengthens friendships. It improves support systems. It gives communities order during moments that could otherwise create disorder. Planning shapes communities not only by reducing confusion, but by elevating collective strength.

When planning becomes common within a community, it leaves a legacy that extends far beyond individual families. It becomes part of how the community defines itself. People begin to see preparation as responsible rather than frightening. They see clarity as compassionate rather than uncomfortable. They understand that planning protects the emotional health of everyone involved. This legacy influences future generations. Children grow up watching adults discuss important matters honestly. Young adults adopt the habits they witnessed. Elders pass down traditions of clarity and responsibility. Over time, each generation becomes more confident and more prepared than the one before.

Every person contributes to the world they leave behind. They shape the emotional environment. They shape traditions. They shape expectations. Thoughtful planning shapes that world in a profound way because it teaches care, intention, responsibility, and love expressed through clarity. The world we leave behind is not only built on achievements or possessions. It is built on the emotional imprint of our choices, and planning ahead leaves a world that is calmer, more compassionate, and more unified.

A community is more than a collection of families. It is a shared space where values spread from household to household. When people plan ahead, they contribute to the legacy of the entire community. They help create an environment where peace is possible. They help reduce the emotional burden on others. They help shape a culture in which preparation is seen as an expression of love rather than fear. Communities grow stronger when people take responsibility for their part in them, and planning is one of the clearest ways to do that.

The next chapter will explore the emotional transformation that occurs when people shift from avoidance to empowerment. It will focus on the psychological impact of stepping into clarity and choosing a path that brings peace not only to oneself, but to others as well.

Chapter 11

FROM AVOIDANCE TO EMPOWERMENT

Every person reaches a moment when they realize avoidance no longer serves them. Sometimes it arrives quietly through reflection. Sometimes it comes suddenly after witnessing someone else's struggle. It may follow a health scare. It may follow the loss of a friend. It may come simply with maturity. Whatever the trigger, the moment marks a turning point between fear and strength.

Avoidance is passive. Empowerment is active. Avoidance retreats inward. Empowerment reaches outward. Avoidance narrows perspective. Empowerment expands it. When someone chooses empowerment, they are choosing clarity over fear and intention over uncertainty. While that shift can look like courage from the outside, it is often driven by something even more fundamental: awareness. The journey from avoidance to empowerment is not defined by being fearless. It is defined by seeing clearly.

Avoidance is often misunderstood as irresponsibility. In truth, it is usually fear. Fear of making the wrong decision. Fear of acknowledging mortality. Fear of burdening others. Fear of confronting the unknown. These fears are deeply human. Nearly everyone carries them at some point in life, and for many people they are rooted in care. People avoid the subject because they want to protect themselves from discomfort, and because they want to protect their family from pain. The problem is not that people do not care. The problem is that care becomes misdirected. Silence feels protective, but it often creates the very stress it was meant to prevent.

When people begin to explore these fears without judgment, insight follows. They recognize that fear often comes from a desire for control. They see that the impulse to avoid is often the mind's attempt to keep life feeling safe and predictable. And once they understand that, the fear becomes easier to hold. It becomes something they can face rather than something they must obey. Avoidance stops being a character flaw and becomes an opportunity for growth.

Awareness is the beginning of emotional courage. Courage does not appear suddenly. It grows as people see what avoidance has cost them. They recognize the stress it created. They recognize the confusion it caused. They recognize the pressure it placed on others. This awareness becomes a catalyst. It does not eliminate fear, but it changes the relationship with fear. Instead of letting fear dictate action, people acknowledge it and choose clarity anyway. That choice is empowerment. It is the moment someone takes responsibility not because they are fearless, but because they are aware.

Empowerment rarely begins with one dramatic leap. It usually begins with small steps. A conversation with a loved one. A preference stated out loud. A moment of reflection. A single document completed. These steps may not look significant, yet they build confidence. Each step proves to the person that they can handle what once felt overwhelming. Each step reduces fear. Each step strengthens clarity. Many people describe a surprising sense of pride when they begin planning. They feel capable. They feel grounded. They feel closer to their values. Small actions create momentum, and momentum becomes empowerment.

This shift has a real effect on emotional health. People who step into clarity often describe feeling lighter. Anxiety decreases. The mind feels less scattered. Life feels more organized. There is a greater sense of control, not over death itself but over what will be left behind. People feel aligned with purpose. They take responsibility not from obligation, but from care. Empowerment does not remove life's challenges, but it reshapes the way challenges are approached. It moves people out of helplessness and into intention.

Empowerment also changes relationships. When someone moves from avoidance to empowerment, communication often becomes more open. They talk more honestly about their wishes. They invite conversations with family members who may have avoided the subject as well. They show vulnerability, and that vulnerability gives others permission to be honest too. These conversations build trust. They deepen understanding. They help families align expectations. Empowerment creates emotional maturity. It reduces the tension silence creates. It replaces uncertainty with clarity. When someone takes ownership of planning, they demonstrate care in a way that strengthens every relationship connected to them. Empowered action becomes a stabilizing force in the family.

It also tends to spread. Empowerment is contagious. When one person confronts fear and creates a plan, others notice. They see the peace it brings. They see the strength it creates. They see the confidence that follows. Family members often follow the example. Friends ask questions. Colleagues become curious. Empowered behavior breaks stigma and weakens the silence that keeps people stuck. It gives others permission to act with the same clarity. In this way, empowerment becomes a gift not only to the individual, but to everyone around them. One person's shift can inspire many.

Empowerment transforms the experience of mortality itself. Avoidance keeps mortality in the shadows, which makes it feel darker and more overwhelming. Empowerment brings the subject into the light, making it feel manageable. It encourages reflection rather than denial. It opens space for meaning instead of fear. People who embrace empowerment often describe an unexpected transformation. They appreciate life more deeply. They become more intentional with their time. They strengthen relationships. They express gratitude more often. They focus on the values they want to carry forward. Empowerment turns mortality into a reminder of how important it is to live fully.

One of the greatest benefits of empowerment is the relief it gives to loved ones. Families are not left guessing about preferences. They are not forced to debate decisions without direction. They are not required to carry the emotional burden of uncertainty. Empowerment protects the people who remain. It leaves clarity, direction, and peace in a moment that could otherwise be defined by confusion. This protection becomes part of a person's legacy.

Once someone experiences the clarity empowerment provides, they rarely return to avoidance. They maintain their plan. They update it. They refine it. They revisit it as life changes. Empowerment becomes a foundation rather than a moment. That foundation can shape generations. Children who watch adults plan grow up feeling more comfortable doing the same. Grandchildren inherit a family culture where planning is normal. A strong foundation of empowerment supports decades of clarity and stability.

There is also a deeper truth here: Avoidance can feel like freedom, but it is often limitation. It keeps people from facing reality. It keeps them from making choices. It keeps them from expressing wishes. It keeps them from shaping a legacy. Empowerment is true freedom. It allows people to speak openly. It allows them to define what matters. It allows them to control their narrative and create peace for themselves and others. Empowerment gives people ownership over the part of life that many feel powerless to approach. It is freedom shaped through intention.

This shift also redefines responsibility. Responsibility is often misunderstood as a burden, but empowerment reframes it. When someone takes responsibility willingly, they feel stronger rather than weighed down. They feel purposeful rather than pressured. They feel aligned rather than conflicted. What once felt overwhelming becomes meaningful. What once felt frightening becomes manageable. What once felt like something to avoid becomes something that reflects care and maturity. Responsibility becomes an expression of love.

The journey does not end with planning. The movement from avoidance to empowerment influences the way people live. They become more intentional with decisions. They speak more honestly. They take ownership of actions. They choose what aligns with values. Empowerment becomes a model for living, extending into work, relationships, health, and personal growth. It becomes an internal compass. The person no longer reacts from fear, but acts from awareness, and that awareness shapes everything they touch.

Planning, in the end, is not merely a task. It is a transformation. It takes people from silence to communication. From uncertainty to clarity. From fear to confidence. From heaviness to peace. It strengthens families, communities, and personal identity. Empowerment is the heart of that transformation. It is the moment someone steps forward with intention and chooses a path that brings peace to themselves and to the people they love.

The next chapter will explore the deeper meaning of living with clarity. It will examine how planning influences day-to-day life and how a thoughtful relationship with mortality can enhance the experience of being alive. Empowerment is not the end of the journey; it is the beginning of living with purpose.

Chapter 12

LIVING WITH CLARITY

Clarity is not only something people experience after planning. It becomes a way of moving through the world. When someone embraces clarity, decisions begin to carry more intention. Words become more honest. Time is treated with greater respect. Relationships are approached with deeper care. Clarity stops being something a person completes and becomes something a person lives.

Living with clarity creates a sense of grounding. People become less reactive and less overwhelmed. They focus on what matters instead of getting tangled in what does not. Clarity simplifies the emotional landscape. It removes noise that distracts the mind. It brings a calm sense of direction that influences every part of life. Living with clarity is living with purpose.

One of the first changes clarity brings is a new relationship with time. Many people move through life assuming they have endless time. They postpone meaningful conversations. They delay important decisions. They tell themselves they will live more intentionally later. But clarity reveals something most people know intellectually and rarely feel emotionally: Time is not something to take for granted; it is something to use wisely.

When someone embraces clarity, time becomes more valuable because it becomes more real. People become more present. They waste less energy on conflict or avoidable stress.

They use time to strengthen relationships. They invest in experiences that matter. They spend more time with the people they love. They begin to treat time as sacred, not because they are afraid but because they understand its worth.

Clarity also encourages thoughtful choices. When life is approached without intention, decisions are often made reactively. People respond to pressure. They say yes when they want to say no. They avoid discomfort rather than face it. Clarity shifts this pattern by inviting a pause. It creates a space between impulse and action. It encourages people to choose based on values rather than fear, convenience, or expectation.

Thoughtful choices create consistency. They build a life aligned with internal beliefs. They create integrity. People feel more at peace with themselves when they live in a way that matches what they truly value. Clarity becomes a guide for behavior, not through rigid rules, but through a quiet internal sense of what is true.

This is why clarity strengthens personal identity. Many people move through life without examining what truly matters to them. They follow routines. They adopt beliefs from their surroundings. They make decisions based on expectations rather than personal values. Planning, especially planning that requires people to reflect on mortality, interrupts that autopilot. It invites the questions people often avoid: What do I believe? What do I want? How do I want to be remembered?

That kind of introspection strengthens identity. People begin to understand themselves more deeply. They become clearer about values, priorities, and purpose. Once those things are clear, daily life changes. Decisions become easier. Boundaries become healthier. The person becomes less pulled by noise and more guided by meaning. Personal identity becomes stronger when it is examined rather than assumed.

Clarity also creates healthier relationships. Relationships thrive when communication is open, when expectations are understood, and when intentions are shared. Clarity encourages these qualities because it requires honest conversations about topics many families avoid. Once those conversations begin, they rarely stay confined to end-of-life planning. People often discover a new ability to speak plainly about needs, hopes, fears, and love.

They share feelings more freely. They listen with greater compassion. They allow vulnerability because clarity has taught them that transparency strengthens relationships rather than weakens them. Healthy relationships grow from authentic communication, and living with clarity makes authenticity feel natural instead of risky.

As clarity grows, emotional overwhelm begins to shrink. Many people carry quiet emotional weight: unresolved responsibilities, unspoken worries, a background fear of what would happen if something unexpected occurred. These concerns create stress that lingers beneath daily life. People may not talk about it, but they feel it.

When someone embraces clarity, that overwhelm begins to dissolve. The fear of leaving unfinished business lessens. The worry about burdening loved ones softens. The quiet tension created by avoidance starts to lift. Clarity replaces that tension with stability, and emotional clarity becomes emotional peace.

Clarity also helps people live with fewer regrets. Regret often comes from choices not made, conversations avoided, opportunities missed. Clarity pushes people to address what matters before time slips away. It encourages people to say what they want loved ones to hear. It motivates repair where repair is needed. It inspires prioritization of what truly matters.

People who live with clarity experience fewer regrets because they face important matters directly. They understand that life is unpredictable, and they refuse to postpone what is meaningful. They choose honesty over hesitation. They choose intention over avoidance. Clarity becomes a safeguard against regret because it keeps people awake to the reality that later is never guaranteed.

The same awareness that reduces regret often increases gratitude. Planning forces people to acknowledge mortality, and once that truth is understood deeply, it becomes difficult to take life for granted. People who embrace clarity often describe a growing appreciation for ordinary moments. They notice the small things. They value time with loved ones more. They express gratitude more frequently.

Gratitude shifts emotional perspective. It brings joy. It reduces stress. It increases resilience. It strengthens relationships. Clarity makes gratitude a natural part of daily life, because gratitude grows when life is viewed through the lens of intention.

Clarity also makes room for personal growth. Avoidance keeps people stuck. It blocks emotional development and limits self-understanding. When someone chooses clarity, they break through those barriers. They face truths that once felt overwhelming. They learn about themselves. They grow stronger.

That growth extends beyond planning. It changes how someone handles conflict. It shapes decision-making. It influences how adversity is met. It expands the ability to communicate honestly. It builds confidence in the capacity to navigate difficult experiences. Clarity becomes a foundation for ongoing growth, not because life becomes easy, but because the person becomes steadier.

As people become steadier, the way they show love changes too. Love is expressed through presence, protection, responsibility, honesty, and care. When someone embraces clarity, love becomes more intentional. People communicate openly. They plan carefully because they want to protect the people they care about. They speak with more tenderness. They offer more attention. Clarity removes ambiguity and builds trust, deepening emotional bonds. Love becomes stronger when expressed with intention.

This is also how clarity creates a calmer future. People who live with clarity do not pretend they can control every outcome. Instead, they create stability where it is possible. They make choices that reduce chaos. They prepare realistically. They communicate wishes openly. They remove unnecessary stress from the people they love.

That preparation creates calm for everyone involved. Families are not left guessing. They are not left searching. They are not left confused. They inherit a path rather than a maze. The calm that clarity creates becomes part of a family's emotional landscape. Clarity today becomes peace tomorrow.

Over time, living with clarity transforms the experience of life itself. People become more present, responsible, expressive, grateful, connected, and grounded. They build stronger relationships. They create deeper meaning. They live with less fear and more purpose. This transformation is not sudden. It grows from small moments of awareness, from conversations that matter, and from the courage to look directly at what others avoid. It grows from the understanding that clarity is not about planning for death. It is about improving life.

Clarity, in the end, is a daily choice. It is not achieved once. It is chosen repeatedly: in how people speak, how they act, how they prioritize, how they plan, how they show love, and how they respond to uncertainty. People who embrace clarity learn to nurture it. They update their plans. They reflect on values. They communicate honestly. They make thoughtful decisions. They do this not because it is required, but because it enriches life. Clarity becomes a guiding principle rather than an isolated moment.

That is the deeper meaning of living with clarity. It is not organization for its own sake. It is not paperwork. It is not administration. The deeper meaning is emotional truth. It is connection. It is peace. It is legacy. It is living fully while preparing responsibly. It is understanding that time is finite and relationships matter. It is recognizing that love is expressed not only in words, but in actions that protect others.

When someone chooses clarity, they shape both life and legacy. They choose to live with purpose. They choose to protect the people they love. They choose to face life openly rather than quietly avoiding what they fear. Clarity is a way of honoring life.

Chapter 13

THE COURAGE TO TALK ABOUT DEATH

Talking about death is one of the most avoided conversations in modern life. People will talk about finances. They will talk about relationships. They will talk about work stress. But the moment death enters the room, something shifts. The energy changes. The conversation tightens. People change the topic, make a joke, or look away. That discomfort is universal, and it is deeply human.

The difficulty usually comes from fear. People fear sadness. They fear vulnerability. They fear upsetting someone they love. They fear sounding morbid. They fear the reminder that life has an end. So the subject is treated like a doorway we walk past without opening. Silence becomes the default. Yet silence does not protect anyone. It simply leaves families unprepared and emotionally exposed when loss eventually arrives. The courage to talk about death is the courage to face truth with honesty and compassion.

Many people avoid the conversation because they believe they are sparing themselves, or sparing others, from discomfort. They imagine the discussion might create conflict or sadness. They fear the weight of the topic, so they postpone it. Then they postpone it again. Often they postpone it until the conversation is needed but no longer possible.

Avoidance does not protect families. It places them directly in the center of uncertainty during one of the most painful moments of their lives. When someone dies without sharing wishes, loved ones are left to guess. They debate. They stress. They worry they are making the wrong decisions. They wonder if they are honoring the person or failing them. That turmoil can linger for years, sometimes for generations, not because the family did not care, but because the family did not have clarity. Talking about death is uncomfortable. Avoiding the conversation is far more painful.

The courage to talk about death does not require a dramatic speech. It begins with a single honest moment. A question. A reflection. A simple statement of intention. Small moments like these open a door that has been locked for too long. People often discover something surprising once they step through it: After the first moment of honesty passes, the rest becomes easier. The conversation shifts from fear to clarity, from tension to relief, from silence to understanding. What once felt impossible becomes, over time, natural. Courage grows with each sentence spoken.

When people engage in open conversations about death, relationships often become stronger. These conversations require vulnerability, and vulnerability demands trust. They create space for emotional honesty that many families rarely reach in day-to-day life. People share fears. They share beliefs. They share wishes. They share values and in doing so, they become more real to one another.

These conversations can bring families closer because they reduce assumptions and eliminate misunderstandings. They create an emotional foundation that supports everyone involved. When someone expresses wishes clearly, it becomes a gift to the people who love them. Talking about death can strengthen the bonds that matter most.

Conversation also creates emotional preparedness. Death is inevitable, and the emotional shock of losing someone cannot be avoided entirely. But the chaos that often follows can be reduced dramatically. When families talk openly about wishes, preferences, and values, they become more prepared for what will eventually happen. Preparedness is not about expecting death. It is about understanding that clarity eases suffering. When people know what a loved one wants, they can focus on grieving rather than guessing. They can find comfort in honoring wishes rather than worrying whether they made the right choices. Conversation reduces emotional burden and increases emotional resilience.

It also helps families understand one another more deeply. Many people assume they already know what their loved ones would want. They assume they understand beliefs and preferences. Yet when these conversations finally happen, people are often surprised. They hear ideas they never expected. They learn about fears and hopes that were never shared. They discover values that had gone unspoken for years. Talking about death becomes a way of seeing the people we love more clearly. It reveals what matters most to them. It clarifies priorities. It opens space for questions and reflection. Families who have these conversations often describe more closeness and more mutual respect afterward. Understanding begins with conversation.

Honesty also reduces conflict during grief. Grief creates strain. People are vulnerable, exhausted, overwhelmed. When a family must make major decisions in that state without clear guidance, disagreements can emerge quickly. Even small details can become sources of tension, because the emotions underneath them are so large. But when a loved one has expressed wishes clearly, the family is protected. There is no debate about preferences. There is no uncertainty about intentions. There is no need to negotiate out of fear or frustration. Honesty creates harmony at a time when it is most needed. Talking about death now reduces conflict later.

The conversation does not need to be perfect. Many people avoid talking about death because they feel they need to say everything the right way. They believe there is a perfect opening line. They worry about choosing the wrong moment. They fear being misunderstood. That pressure becomes an excuse to stay silent. The truth is simpler: The conversation does not have to be perfect. It only has to begin. It can start in a quiet moment. It can start with curiosity. It can start with a simple question. It can even start with humor. What matters is that the door opens and the silence breaks. Imperfection is not a barrier. It is part of being human.

When someone chooses to talk openly about death, they also create a legacy of openness. They set an example that honesty is not something to fear. They show that vulnerability can be strength. They demonstrate that difficult topics can be faced with grace and compassion. This example influences others. Family members learn from it. Friends remember it. Future generations carry it forward. Courage becomes a guiding light that outlives the person who first demonstrated it. Openness becomes a generational gift.

Conversation also makes planning possible. Planning cannot happen without words. Someone must speak their wishes, share values, and explain intentions. When the conversation begins, planning becomes natural. It becomes a continuation of honesty. It becomes a shared process rather than a solitary task. Talking about death creates clarity. Clarity creates confidence. Confidence makes planning easier. Families who talk openly often find planning becomes meaningful rather than frightening. It becomes a way to honor life rather than focus on loss. Conversation is the doorway to preparation.

Facing the truth brings emotional freedom. Avoiding death keeps people emotionally constrained. They carry silent fear. They carry unspoken questions. They carry tension they never confront. But when someone speaks openly about death, something loosens. They release burdens they may not have realized they were carrying. They feel lighter, more grounded, more emotionally free. Freedom comes from acknowledging reality. Freedom comes from facing truth. Freedom comes from taking responsibility for the things that matter. Courage leads to emotional freedom.

Ironically, talking about death also helps people live more fully. These conversations often inspire gratitude. They encourage intention. They sharpen awareness of what matters. People prioritize relationships. They appreciate time. They focus on meaning. Those who face mortality openly often describe feeling more alive. They do not dwell on fear. They focus on purpose. They treat life as something to savor rather than something to rush through. In that way, facing death helps people embrace life.

At its core, the courage to talk about death is compassion in action. It recognizes that silence places a heavy burden on others. It understands that clarity is a form of protection. It accepts that love sometimes requires difficult conversations. When someone chooses to speak openly, they demonstrate care for their family. They reduce future stress. They prevent confusion. They offer guidance that will matter during one of the hardest moments a family can face. Courage is not only about facing fear. It is about protecting the people we love.

That is why the first conversation matters so much. Once it happens, everything begins to change. Families grow more comfortable discussing important matters. Individuals feel relief. Planning becomes easier. Openness becomes normal. The silence that once surrounded the topic starts to disappear. The first conversation does not need to answer every question. It simply needs to begin the process. Once the door is open, future conversations become natural and meaningful. Every journey toward clarity begins with a single moment of courage.

In the end, talking about death is not only about death; it is about love. Love expressed through honesty. Love expressed through responsibility. Love expressed through clarity. Love expressed through preparation. When people talk about death, they are really talking about how they want to protect their families, ease emotional burdens, and preserve what matters most. These conversations reveal the deepest priorities of a life. Talking about death is a profound act of love.

Chapter 14

THE HEALING POWER
OF PREPARATION

Many people believe healing begins only after loss, as if healing is something reserved for the season of grief. But healing can begin long before loss ever occurs. Preparation itself becomes a powerful form of healing because it invites reflection, reduces fear, strengthens relationships, and allows people to face mortality in a way that brings peace rather than turmoil.

Preparation is not a cold administrative task. It is emotional work. It is the act of finding grounding in a truth that is easy to avoid and hard to control. When someone prepares, they acknowledge the weight of life. They recognize the importance of relationships. They consider the people they love with care and intention. That act alone creates space for healing long before grief arrives. Preparation becomes an early step in emotional resilience.

Avoidance may feel protective in the moment, but it often creates stress beneath the surface. People who avoid planning carry quiet worry. They fear the unknown. They fear leaving chaos behind. They fear the emotional strain their family may experience. Those fears do not disappear simply because they are ignored. They linger, shaping the background of daily life.

Preparation invites people to face reality gently. It allows someone to approach the topic at their own pace, without panic and without pressure. It transforms the unknown into something understandable. And when reality is faced calmly and intentionally, emotional discomfort begins to soften. That softness is the beginning of healing. Healing begins with truth approached with compassion.

Life also becomes stressful when thoughts are scattered, when tasks remain undone, when important conversations linger unspoken, and when responsibilities weigh on the mind. Disorganization creates emotional tension that builds over time. Many people carry it as heaviness, as mental clutter, as an uneasy sense that something important is being avoided.

Preparation helps organize not just documents, but emotions and responsibilities. It creates structure where there was none. It turns confusion into clarity. It gives people a sense of control over matters that once felt overwhelming. That organization allows the mind to rest. Anxiety decreases. Emotional space opens. In this way, emotional organization is healing.

One of the most powerful sources of healing comes from knowing loved ones will not be left overwhelmed. Many people fear becoming a burden. They worry about leaving confusion behind. They worry about family members navigating grief while also carrying countless decisions. These concerns can create discomfort that lingers quietly for years.

Preparation reduces that burden dramatically. When someone completes their plans, relief follows. They know their family will have guidance. They know wishes are clear. They know they have left peace rather than chaos. That knowledge creates comfort and emotional freedom. Healing grows when the heart feels lighter.

Preparation also invites reflection and meaning. When people consider how they want to be remembered, they begin to examine their lives. They think about values. They think about relationships. They think about what matters most. This reflection often reveals meaning that was overlooked in the rush of daily life. People discover gratitude. They rediscover purpose. They see life with a new perspective. They recognize achievements both large and small. Reflection heals because it reconnects people with their own story in a gentle, meaningful way. It is not about dwelling on endings. It is about appreciating the fullness of life.

Preparation naturally leads to conversations that might otherwise be avoided. These conversations are not always easy, but they matter. They open the door to emotional honesty. They allow families to share thoughts that have been quietly carried. They create moments of vulnerability that strengthen connection. People express love more openly. They speak about fears. They share wishes. They ask questions they have never asked. They listen with more patience. Speaking honestly becomes healing in itself because it removes emotional distance, creates unity, and fosters understanding. Healing happens when truth replaces silence.

Preparation also creates emotional preparedness. Grief will always bring sadness. It is the natural response to losing someone we love. But emotional chaos does not need to accompany that sadness. Preparation allows families to enter grief with stability. They are not blindsided by uncertainty. They are not forced into rapid decisions. They are not searching for answers during the hardest moments of their lives. Emotional preparedness does not remove grief. It gives grief space to exist without being overshadowed by stress. It allows families to focus on love rather than logistics, to grieve with dignity rather than confusion. Preparation softens the emotional impact of grief.

As preparation continues, fear often begins to release. Fear of the unknown. Fear of leaving others unprepared. Fear of confronting mortality. Fear of emotional pain. When people plan, they meet these fears gradually, and they learn an important truth: Fear loses strength when it is faced directly. With each step, the subject feels less overwhelming. Planning becomes manageable. Clarity brings peace. As fear fades, calm emerges, and that calm is deeply healing because it replaces tension with acceptance. Healing expands when fear recedes.

Purposeful action is another form of healing. Taking action gives people a sense of purpose because it is not simply completing tasks. It is acting with intention. It is taking ownership of the future. It is protecting the people we love. It is creating meaning through responsibility. Purposeful action builds confidence. It reduces anxiety. It reinforces personal strength. It connects people to values. Agency is healing, because even in matters we cannot fully control, we can still create clarity and stability. Purpose heals the heart.

Peace of mind may be the most profound form of healing preparation provides. Peace of mind settles the mind. It relaxes the body. It eases emotional tension. It allows people to live with less fear and more presence. Preparation creates peace of mind because it resolves unanswered questions. It provides direction. It gives confidence that someone has done right by the people they love. This peace carries into daily life. People sleep better. They worry less. They feel more organized and more connected to what matters. Healing becomes sustainable when peace of mind is present.

Preparation also encourages acceptance. It does not force people to dwell on death. It simply helps people understand mortality as a natural part of life. When someone accepts this truth, anxiety often decreases. Acceptance does not eliminate sadness. It removes the fear that makes sadness harder to bear. Acceptance allows people to appreciate life more fully. They focus on what matters. They embrace meaningful experiences. They communicate openly. They express love without hesitation. Healing is rooted in acceptance of life's reality.

When plans are complete, they create a legacy of clarity for the family. That clarity reduces distress, prevents conflict, provides direction, and brings comfort during loss. In that way, it continues to heal long after the person is gone. Families who inherit clarity often feel supported and connected. They feel guided when guidance is needed most. This legacy becomes part of the family's emotional story, strengthening future generations. Healing continues through the legacy preparation creates.

Ironically, preparing for the end often brings people closer to life. They become more present. They appreciate small joys. They prioritize relationships. They cherish time. Preparation becomes a reminder not of death, but of how important it is to live well. This connection to life is healing because it enriches each day. It encourages gratitude, inspires purpose, and creates balance. Preparation invites a deeper connection to life itself.

Healing, in the end, is not a single event. It is an ongoing journey. Preparation is part of that journey. It begins with reflection. It continues with conversation. It grows through action. It expands through emotional understanding. It becomes part of how people experience both life and loss. This journey shapes the way people relate to themselves and to others. It builds resilience, perspective, and peace. Healing becomes a natural outcome of living with clarity and intention.

The next chapter will explore how preparation supports families long after someone has passed and how clarity continues to guide those left behind.

Chapter 15

How Clarity Supports Families after Loss

When a loved one dies, the first hours are often a blur. Shock sets in. Emotions collide. The mind struggles to process what has happened. Even when a loss is expected, the moment itself can feel surreal. In those early hours, families rarely think clearly. They move through tasks mechanically. They rely on instinct. They feel heavy and unsteady, as if the ground beneath them has shifted.

Without clarity, those first hours can become chaotic. Family members may disagree about what to do next. They may search frantically for documents. They may panic about decisions they never expected to make. They may fear doing something wrong, fear choosing something that cannot be undone, fear making a mistake that will haunt them later. All of this happens while they are still trying to comprehend the emotional weight of the loss.

But when clarity exists, the experience changes. There is direction. There is structure. There is guidance. Families can focus on their emotions rather than scrambling for information. This is one of the greatest gifts planning provides. Clarity becomes an anchor during one of the most disorienting moments of their lives.

In the days following a death, many families carry an unspoken fear of making mistakes. They worry about choosing the wrong funeral arrangements. They worry about unintentionally going against the person's wishes. They worry about disappointing other family members. These worries create emotional turmoil that can complicate grief, turning sadness into pressure and love into anxiety.

Clear instructions remove these fears. When a family knows exactly what their loved one wanted, relief follows. They do not have to guess. They do not have to debate. They do not have to carry the burden of deciding what is "right." They can simply follow the guidance the person offered. That clarity lifts a significant emotional weight at a time when even small decisions can feel overwhelming.

Clarity also minimizes conflict. Loss brings deep emotions to the surface, and even the closest families can experience tension during grief because everyone processes differently. Without guidance, small disagreements can escalate into larger fractures. People argue about funeral details. They interpret memories differently. They believe they are honoring the person, even while moving in opposite directions.

When wishes are documented and shared, those conflicts are often prevented before they begin. The plan becomes the guiding voice. It replaces debate with direction. It reduces the strain that uncertainty creates. Instead of defending opinions, family members can focus on supporting one another. Clarity fosters harmony during a time when unity matters most.

Perhaps the most overlooked truth about loss is that grief requires space: emotional space, mental space, even physical space. When families are overwhelmed by decisions, there is no room left to grieve. Attention is divided. Hearts are pulled in too many directions. Preparation protects that space. It allows families to cry, sit together, reflect, comfort one another, and feel the loss without the constant pressure of unanswered questions. Clarity gives families permission to grieve naturally.

Clarity also honors the life that was lived. When someone's wishes are clear, the family experiences a deep sense of respect for that person's identity. They can honor preferences, traditions, and personality. The funeral or celebration of life becomes a true reflection, not a hurried approximation built from assumptions. That authenticity brings comfort. It helps families feel they are doing something meaningful. It supports healing through ritual and helps people stay connected to the one they are saying goodbye to. Clarity ensures the final chapter reflects the life with accuracy and love.

After the service, another reality arrives: the administrative overload. Families are confronted with a mountain of tasks. Accounts must be closed. Institutions must be notified. Bills must be located. Insurance must be processed. Legal responsibilities must be addressed. For many families, this burden feels crushing because it arrives when emotional strength is at its lowest.

When information has been prepared ahead of time, the burden is dramatically reduced. Loved ones can locate important details quickly. They know which accounts exist. They know which policies are in place. They know who needs to be contacted and what steps to take. Clear organization prevents unnecessary stress and eliminates hours of searching. Clarity simplifies responsibilities during a period when simplicity matters greatly.

Clarity also gives loved ones something grief rarely provides on its own: confidence. When families must guess, they often carry doubt for years. They wonder if they made the right decisions. They replay conversations trying to interpret hints. That lingering uncertainty can complicate grief in lasting ways.

Clarity removes doubt. It allows people to feel secure in their actions and proud of the care they provided. They can grieve without the added ache of "Did we do the right thing?"

Confidence becomes a quiet comfort that supports healing long after the funeral has passed.

In many cases, clarity preserves family bonds. Loss can strain families or bring them closer. When no plan exists, stress rises, emotions flare, resentments can surface, and relationships that were once strong may become damaged by conflict and pressure. When clarity is provided, families often experience the opposite. They feel united. They work together with purpose. The plan becomes a shared guide that aligns them. Instead of arguing, they support one another. This unity becomes part of how the family remembers the person who passed. Clarity protects relationships during one of the most vulnerable times a family can face.

Clarity supports healthy grieving for another reason: It changes how grief begins. Healthy grieving requires grounding and time. When the early days after a death are filled with rushed decisions and uncertainty, people step into grief from exhaustion instead of presence. That exhaustion can prolong emotional strain and make healing harder. Clarity offers a different beginning. Families enter grief with answers instead of questions, direction instead of confusion. They are not scrambling. They are not overwhelmed by uncertainty. They are simply grieving the way human beings are meant to grieve. Healthy grieving begins with clarity.

Many families also describe something subtle but profound when a plan exists: a sense of continued connection. When a loved one leaves behind clear instructions, it can feel as though they are still communicating. Preferences speak for them. Instructions feel like messages of love. Choices feel personal and intentional. Families often say they feel guided and supported, even in the absence of the person. That connection softens the emotional weight of separation. Clarity becomes a bridge between the one who has passed and the ones who remain.

Clarity protects families financially as well. Financial confusion can add unnecessary hardship after a death. Families may not know where accounts are held. They may not understand insurance policies. They may not know which subscriptions must be canceled. They may face unexpected bills or legal complications. Preparation prevents many of these issues. It organizes information, clarifies responsibilities, and reduces stress. It ensures resources are used wisely and allows the family to focus on emotional healing rather than financial confusion.

Over time, clarity strengthens legacy. A person's legacy is shaped not only by what they did in life, but by the emotional environment they leave behind. When families experience a peaceful, organized transition, they remember the person with gratitude. They speak about thoughtfulness. They feel the care that guided them. That becomes part of how the person is remembered. Clarity creates a legacy of peace rather than chaos, and it often inspires future generations to plan with the same intention.

Clarity can even reduce trauma. Sudden or unprepared loss can feel traumatic, and that shock intensifies when families have no direction. They feel lost. They feel overwhelmed. They feel thrust into decisions they never anticipated. When a plan exists, the shock is still real, but the trauma is often reduced. Families feel held by structure. They move through the first stage of loss with grounding rather than panic. Clarity becomes a stabilizing force during emotional upheaval.

It also allows families to honor the person with confidence. A meaningful farewell is one of the most important parts of healing. When families know what their loved one wanted, they can create a ceremony that truly reflects the individual. They are not guessing. They are fulfilling a wish. That confidence brings comfort and supports closure. Grief becomes a loving tribute rather than a confused struggle. Clarity creates ceremonies rooted in authenticity and respect.

The benefits of clarity do not end after the first week, or even the first year. Families continue to feel its impact for years. They remember how guided they felt. They feel grateful for the thoughtfulness that was shown. They experience fewer regrets. They often feel a stronger bond with the person who planned ahead. This peace becomes part of the family's emotional story. It influences how they approach their own planning. It becomes a tradition of responsibility and care. When clarity continues to guide families long after a loss, it becomes a legacy of love.

Chapter 16

GRIEF WITH DIRECTION VERSUS GRIEF IN CHAOS

Grief is universal. Anyone who has loved someone will eventually experience it. But while grief is shared, the way people move through it can look very different. Some families enter grief with clarity. Others enter grief in confusion. The emotional difference between those two paths is profound. When clarity exists, grief is still painful, but it is grounded. When chaos exists, grief becomes overwhelming and disorienting.

These two paths often shape how long grief feels consuming, how deeply it affects a family, and how quickly healing can begin. Grief with direction feels supported. Grief in chaos feels isolating. The loss is the same, but the experience is not. The presence or absence of clarity often sets the tone for the entire grieving journey.

When families have clear guidance, grief unfolds with a kind of emotional steadiness. They know what needs to be done. They understand the person's wishes. They have a blueprint that can carry them through the most difficult days. That sense of direction reduces fear. It reduces stress. It reduces the emotional overload uncertainty creates.

Grief with direction does not eliminate sadness. It does not remove tears, longing, or heartbreak. But it allows those emotions to move freely rather than getting tangled in confusion. It gives the heart space to feel without feeling lost. It allows families to focus on love instead of logistics. In this way, direction becomes emotional grounding.

When families have no guidance, grief becomes tangled with anxiety. Every decision becomes a source of stress. Every family member may carry a different interpretation of what the "right" choice should be. Decisions that should take minutes can take days. Small disagreements become emotional battles. Every step feels heavy.

The chaos does not come from the loss itself. It comes from the lack of clarity surrounding the loss. Families feel unprepared. They feel overwhelmed. They feel frightened of making mistakes. They move through early grief carrying a burden they were never meant to carry. Chaos intensifies grief and prolongs suffering.

This is one reason chaos makes grief harder to heal. Healing requires space. Families need the freedom to cry, to sit quietly, to talk, to remember, to process. When chaos surrounds a loss, these emotional needs are squeezed out by pressure. The mind becomes focused on tasks rather than mourning. Instead of being allowed to grieve, people are forced into constant decision-making.

Chaos also creates guilt. Family members worry they did something wrong. They regret decisions made under pressure. They wonder if they honored the person properly. These unresolved emotions become heavy and persistent, and they can prolong grief by keeping the mind trapped in second-guessing. Chaos turns grief into an emotional storm, and storms are not environments where healing happens easily.

Clarity changes the emotional rhythm of grief. It gives families a starting point. It gives them guidance. It gives them confidence. When they know they are following their loved one's wishes, they experience a deeper sense of peace. They move through early grief with fewer doubts. They can focus on comforting one another rather than interpreting what the person might have wanted.

Clarity also creates emotional safety. Families understand they are not navigating the loss alone. They feel supported by the person's own words and decisions. That safety allows grief to unfold naturally rather than inside psychological distress. Clarity is not a cure for grief, but it is a support system for healing.

Structure plays an essential role during emotional upheaval. Grief asks the mind to process intense emotion while also trying to handle practical decisions, and that combination can feel impossible. When a clear plan exists, structure steps in. Tasks become straightforward. Decisions are predetermined. Steps follow one another naturally. Families do not have to invent solutions while grieving. They do not have to negotiate every detail. They can move forward with purpose instead of uncertainty. In that sense, structure becomes a form of compassion.

Direction also reduces family conflict. Loss makes people emotionally fragile. They are more sensitive. Memories carry more weight. Differences in opinion can quickly become disagreements. Without guidance, families may argue about funeral details or interpret wishes differently. Even loving families can experience tension during grief. Direction removes the source of these conflicts. When a plan exists, family members share a reference point. They follow the same guidance. They trust the same document. Unity becomes easier because the burden of interpretation is removed. Direction protects the family from unnecessary emotional wounds.

Regret is one of the most painful emotions connected to grief, and chaos often creates the conditions where regret thrives. When families make decisions without guidance, they revisit those choices long after the funeral. They ask if they did the right thing. They wonder if they missed something important. They carry uncertainty about how they handled the moment. Chaos amplifies regret because the lack of clarity leaves doubt behind. Those regrets can linger for years and complicate healing.

When clarity exists, regret has far less room to grow. Families know they honored the person accurately. They know their actions were rooted in respect. They know they followed expressed intentions. Clarity brings emotional resolution that chaos cannot provide.

Over the long term, grief with direction often leads to a healthier emotional outcome. Families remember the loss with sadness, but also with peace. They recall how supported they felt. They remember unity. They feel gratitude for the guidance that was left behind. Years later, they still appreciate the clarity that carried them through. It becomes part of the story they tell about the person. It becomes part of the person's legacy. It even shapes how they approach their own planning. Clarity shapes memories as much as it shapes decisions.

Grief in chaos can leave scars. Families may remember confusion more vividly than the service itself. They may remember arguments, stress, and decisions they felt unsure about. That turbulence can complicate relationships for years. It can also shape future behavior. Some people vow never to leave their own families in such confusion. Others feel emotionally blocked from discussing planning at all because the subject is tied to pain. Chaos continues to influence families long after the immediate grief has passed, and emotional wounds left by chaos do not heal easily.

Direction also honors the person's story. Every life has a story, and the preferences someone holds at the end reflect the final chapter of that story. When wishes are communicated clearly and carried out faithfully, the story feels complete. It feels intentional. It stays connected to identity. Families are not simply performing tasks; they are honoring meaning and values.

They are respecting traditions and beliefs. They are expressing love through action. Direction turns grief into tribute, and tribute is one of the ways healing begins.

This is why clarity creates emotional strength. Clarity provides confidence during one of the most vulnerable moments of human experience. It reduces panic. It lessens confusion. It gives families room to support one another. Emotional strength is not the absence of sadness. It is the presence of grounding. Families with clarity move through grief with more stability. They communicate better. They comfort one another more easily. They make decisions with less fear. That strength becomes part of the foundation that supports healing, and it strengthens the bonds that hold families together.

Grief with direction is, ultimately, a path toward healing. Healing does not begin when grief ends. Healing begins while grief is still present. Direction creates a path that allows healing to start sooner. Families do not spend the early days untangling confusion. They begin grieving with order and support, and that stability sets the tone for what follows. Grief with direction does not erase pain, but it softens it. It creates safety. It provides reassurance. It gives families room to breathe. Direction is healing in motion.

This leads to the responsibility we carry for those we love. Every person has the ability to influence how their family experiences grief. We can leave confusion, or we can leave clarity. We can force our family to guess, or we can guide them. Approached with intention, this responsibility is not heavy; it is a profound act of love. When someone prepares their wishes, they give their family a gift that cannot be measured. They protect them from emotional overload. They reduce potential conflict. They give confidence. They create a path toward healing. They offer clarity during life's most difficult moment. The responsibility we carry is an opportunity to show love in its most generous form.

Chapter 17

HOW LEGACY CONTINUES TO GUIDE LOVED ONES

Many people think legacy is something fixed, something that becomes permanent the moment a person dies. But legacy is not frozen in time. It lives. It moves. It breathes through the people who remain. Long after a life has ended, legacy continues to shape thoughts, decisions, and the emotional landscape of a family.

A meaningful legacy is not built from possessions, and it is not defined by accomplishments alone. Legacy is shaped by values, memories, lessons, and clarity. When someone leaves behind direction and insight, their influence does not stop. It continues forward as a guiding presence, shaping family identity and emotional well-being. Legacy is not a single moment. It is an ongoing relationship between the past and the present.

After a loss, people often find themselves thinking about the person during important decisions. They ask, what would they have done? They hear their voice in moments of uncertainty. They reach for lessons that were shared over years, sometimes through direct advice, sometimes through quiet example. In this way, legacy becomes a form of guidance.

That influence is subtle, yet powerful. It shows up when someone chooses integrity. When they comfort another person. When they face adversity with courage. When they practice compassion in situations where it would be easier not to. Legacy is carried through actions, not through memory alone. Loved ones become the living expression of the values they inherited.

Legacy also continues through family traditions. Traditions hold emotional history. They contain stories. They shape identity. When someone leaves behind strong traditions, those practices keep guiding the family long after the person is gone. Holiday rituals. Shared meals. Cultural customs. Belief systems. These traditions become reminders of the person's influence.

Families keep traditions alive because they represent connection. They represent continuity. They represent love. When traditions are passed down, they extend a person's presence across generations. A child who never met a grandparent can still feel connected through the customs that carry that grandparent's voice. Traditions become emotional bridges between generations.

Legacy also lives in the way loved ones speak about the person. The stories families tell after a loss shape how someone is remembered. These stories carry personality, humor, wisdom, flaws, and triumphs. They form a shared narrative that will be passed from one generation to the next. When families speak about someone with clarity and affection, legacy becomes stronger and more enduring.

Stories can offer comfort. They can provide guidance. They can help people feel connected in difficult seasons. They become emotional grounding. The way a person is spoken about becomes part of their lasting influence. Legacy is strengthened through storytelling, because storytelling keeps meaning alive.

Often, a legacy includes the emotional qualities a person demonstrated during life. Resilience becomes a model. Courage becomes an example. The way someone navigated hardship becomes a teaching. Families draw strength from these qualities, not as abstract ideas but as practical tools when life becomes difficult. Someone might remember how the person persevered.

Someone might recall their kindness. Someone might think of how they handled adversity with dignity. These memories become resources. Legacy creates resilience that continues long after death.

Legacy is also a source of comfort in hard moments. After a loss, people search for comfort wherever they can find it, and legacy provides comfort in ways that feel personal and intimate. A memory can calm the heart. A lesson once taught can bring reassurance. A phrase the person used to say can steady the mind. Even the recollection of a voice can bring a sense of grounding.

Legacy comforts because it is familiar. It is connected to love rather than fear. It reminds the grieving person that they were shaped by someone who cared deeply for them. That connection softens loneliness. It replaces emotional emptiness with a sense of continued belonging. Comfort becomes a form of healing that legacy makes possible.

When someone leaves behind clear wishes, clarity becomes part of the legacy itself. Loved ones remember the thoughtfulness, the care, and the intention behind the planning. That clarity shapes how they speak about the person and how they understand their values. It reinforces the emotional message the person hoped to leave behind: You were loved, you were protected, you were considered. Because that message arrives during one of life's most difficult moments, it stays. The legacy of clarity echoes through generations.

Legacy can become even more tangible through written and recorded messages. Letters, audio recordings, and videos preserve voice and thought in a way that feels alive. These messages can offer comfort, encouragement, guidance, and love long after the loss. Loved ones return to them during milestones: birthdays, anniversaries, difficult moments, triumphs. The words become a steady presence, a reminder that love can continue to speak even when someone is no longer physically present. The voice of a loved one can guide long after the person is gone.

Legacy does not stop with the immediate circle of grief. Children and grandchildren who may never have known the person directly can still feel their influence. They hear stories. They observe traditions. They inherit values. They learn about strengths, kindness, sacrifices, and character. When a legacy is built on clarity and intention, it becomes a positive force that shapes family identity. It influences how younger generations approach relationships, responsibility, and life planning. Legacy becomes part of the family's foundation.

Legacy can also create meaning from loss. Loss can feel senseless, leaving people searching for meaning where none seems present. Legacy becomes part of the meaning that emerges. It transforms a life into something that continues to influence the living. It gives memory a purpose. It offers emotional context that comforts the people who remain.

Meaning does not remove grief, but it can enrich grief. It allows loved ones to see that connection does not vanish. It continues through what was taught, what was modeled, what was loved, and what was left behind with care. Legacy becomes the way meaning is carried forward. Meaning gives grief a place to rest.

Legacy is also a gentle reminder of shared humanity. It reminds people that life is finite for everyone, that each life has an impact, and that every life leaves a mark. That awareness can shift the way people live. They may become more intentional, more compassionate, more grateful, and more aware of the weight of their choices. Legacy is a quiet teacher. It teaches without forcing. It guides without demanding.

At its core, every legacy is rooted in love. Even when people never articulate their intentions, their impact often reflects the love they carried: the lessons they taught, the comfort they provided, the time they invested, the sacrifices they made. Those expressions become the emotional inheritance left behind.

When someone plans ahead and leaves clarity, love becomes even more visible. It becomes love expressed through responsibility, intention, and protection. That form of love continues guiding loved ones long after the person is no longer physically present. Love is the legacy that never fades.

Over time, legacy becomes a compass. It influences how people approach relationships, challenges, decisions, and the way they move through the world with empathy and strength. Families often discover that the lessons left behind become more meaningful as time passes. The older they grow, the more they understand the wisdom behind the words. The more they face their own struggles, the more they appreciate the guidance they received. Legacy remains a steady companion along life's journey.

This is why a well-planned legacy can be one of the greatest gifts. It is not the result of material wealth or grand achievements. It is the result of clarity, communication, responsibility, and love expressed with intention. When someone takes the time to prepare, they leave behind stability rather than confusion. Peace rather than chaos. Connection rather than emotional distance.

This gift cannot be measured, because it shapes emotions, healing, and memory. It becomes part of how a family moves forward with confidence and grace. A well-planned legacy influences generations and strengthens them. The greatest gift one can leave is clarity wrapped in love.

Chapter 18

THE EMOTIONAL PEACE OF KNOWING YOU HONORED SOMEONE'S WISHES

One of the most powerful forms of peace after a loss comes from a simple certainty: You honored the person's wishes. Loss still brings sadness, longing, and moments of disbelief. But when you know you carried out what they asked for, there is also comfort. A quiet reassurance that you upheld their voice when they could no longer speak.

That peace is not abstract. Families often describe it physically: a release of tightness in the chest, a gentler breath, a calmer mind. Grief still exists, but it is not tangled in doubt. It is not complicated by the fear that you made the wrong decisions. It becomes grief anchored in clarity rather than grief fueled by uncertainty. Honoring someone's wishes becomes emotional steadiness during one of life's heaviest moments.

When families do not know what their loved one wanted, the experience often feels like moving through fog. Every decision becomes a guess, and every guess feels risky. They wonder if they chose the right funeral, the right traditions, the right burial or cremation. They wonder if they handled affairs the way the person would have preferred. Even when decisions are made with love and good intentions, the absence of confirmation can leave a lingering ache.

That uncertainty becomes emotional weight. It can haunt people for years, even decades, because a decision made in good faith can still feel unresolved if no one truly knows what was wanted. Doubt keeps the mind replaying moments instead of moving forward. People get pulled into loops of second-guessing, not because they are dramatic but because the stakes were personal and permanent. The absence of clarity can create wounds that time alone does not always heal.

Clear wishes change the way a family enters grief. When guidance exists, people move with purpose. They feel directed rather than adrift. They sense that the person thought deeply about them and wanted to protect them from confusion. That guidance becomes grounding. It allows families to carry out tasks with confidence instead of fear.

Clear wishes change the energy in the room. Instead of asking, "What should we do?" the family can say, "This is what they wanted." The emotional posture shifts. Stress reduces. Fear loosens its grip. Grief becomes simpler, not because it becomes easier but because uncertainty has been removed from it. Clear wishes are a final act of love.

Honoring those wishes often strengthens emotional connection in the very moments when separation feels most painful. Families sometimes describe it as a final conversation carried out through action. They feel guided. They feel closer rather than farther away. The act of honoring a plan can bring unity because it gives everyone a shared purpose. It reduces conflict. It creates emotional harmony. Honoring wishes becomes a shared act of meaning, and meaning is one of the things that helps grief remain bearable.

Respecting someone's wishes also brings dignity to their story. Final wishes reflect identity. They reveal values, beliefs, personality, and what mattered most. When those wishes are honored, the final chapter feels true to the life that came before it. Families often feel proud when they fulfill them. Proud that they respected the person. Proud that they created a farewell rooted in authenticity. That pride becomes part of healing because it gives the memory a sense of completeness. Respecting wishes is a way of honoring a life fully lived.

Honoring wishes also reduces guilt, which is one of the most common and painful emotions after loss. People worry they did not do enough. They wonder if they made the right choices. They replay moments and wish they had acted differently. But when loved ones know they honored what was clearly expressed, guilt has far less room to grow. They are not haunted by questions because the answers were given. This freedom from guilt allows grief to unfold naturally instead of becoming tangled in regret. Honoring wishes gives people permission to grieve without self-blame.

Clarity protects families from unnecessary conflict as well. When no plan exists, disagreements can emerge quickly. Family members interpret memories differently. Cultural and religious assumptions collide. People debate what is respectful or appropriate, and relationships can strain at the exact time unity is needed most. Clarity removes the source of that conflict. It unites the family under one voice. Instead of debating, people follow what was already laid out. Many families look back with gratitude, not only because the plan helped but because it protected them from discord. Honoring wishes keeps families connected rather than divided.

Clear wishes also deepen the meaning of ritual. Ritual is part of healing. A funeral, a celebration of life, a private moment of remembrance—each one helps people process grief. When someone has expressed how they want to be honored, rituals become more personal and intentional. They feel aligned with the individuality of the person. Families often feel peace because they know the farewell reflects the life. That meaning helps them move into the next stage of grief with greater emotional stability. Ritual becomes a bridge between loss and healing.

Honoring wishes also helps loved ones move forward. Grief is not something people "get over." It becomes part of them. But moving forward requires grounding. When families know they honored their loved one faithfully, they carry fewer doubts and fewer unresolved emotions. They carry less internal conflict. That grounding does not erase pain, but it provides direction. It helps people integrate the loss into life rather than remaining stuck in the earliest stage of grief. Honoring wishes allows healing to gain momentum.

Over time, families reflect on the choices made in those first days. When they know they honored wishes, peace often remains long after the sharpest grief has softened. The memory of fulfilling those wishes becomes a point of comfort. It becomes emotional resolution, a sense that the story was completed with care. This long-term peace protects emotional well-being, and it often shapes future generations. Children grow up hearing how a parent or grandparent planned. They hear how the family honored those plans. Those stories become part of family identity. A completed story offers lasting steadiness.

Clarity continues to reduce emotional burden even years later. Families are less likely to face unexpected complications, unresolved questions, or financial and legal surprises that reopen wounds. Clarity shields them from ongoing stress. It creates space for gratitude rather than regret. It allows the memory of the person to remain clean and peaceful. Clarity is not temporary. It is lasting emotional protection.

Honoring wishes also creates a legacy of respect. When a family follows someone's plan, they establish a precedent. They model that clarity matters. They reinforce that planning deserves respect. Over time, that becomes part of family culture and influences how children and grandchildren approach their own preparation. A legacy of respect strengthens relationships, promotes responsibility, and supports emotional health. Honoring wishes plants seeds that grow into a culture of care.

There is also something tender in the exchange itself. When a person prepares their wishes, they give their family clarity. When the family fulfills those wishes, they give something back. They complete the circle of love and respect. They ensure the person's intentions are honored. They offer a final moment of dignity, even after death. That mutual exchange can feel deeply healing because it affirms connection, strengthens memory, and holds grief alongside gratitude. Honoring wishes is a final act of love that flows in both directions.

Ultimately, the deepest peace comes from knowing you did right by them. You acted with love, integrity, and respect. You did what they asked. You honored their values. You carried out their wishes. That knowledge becomes a steady presence in the heart. It comforts in moments of sadness. It reassures in moments of reflection. It becomes part of the emotional story carried forward. This peace is powerful. It softens grief. It strengthens healing. It remains long after the loss has passed, reminding us that love continues even when a life has ended. Knowing you honored their wishes can bring a peace that stays for a lifetime.

Chapter 19

The Modern Path to End-of-Life Planning

For most of history, end-of-life planning lived in the shadows. It was avoided, scattered, and incomplete. It depended on handwritten notes, lawyer documents tucked into drawers, passwords scribbled on scraps of paper, and assumptions no one ever said out loud. Families often knew little or nothing about a person's wishes until the moment they were forced to guess. And that old approach created exactly what so many families dread: confusion, stress, and an unnecessary emotional burden layered on top of grief.

But the world has changed. People are living longer, and their lives are more complex. There are more financial obligations, more medical decisions, more cultural options, more personal expression, and an entire digital world attached to a person's identity. The planning methods of past generations no longer match modern reality. Planning has entered a new era, and the modern path is rooted in three qualities the old approach rarely provided: clarity, accessibility, and compassion.

Traditional planning often fell short because it was fragmented. A will might be in one place, bank records in another, insurance papers somewhere else, and passwords scattered across notebooks or never written down at all. Funeral wishes might be mentioned casually in a conversation, but never recorded in a way anyone could trust. When loss occurred, families were left searching. They opened drawers. They called attorneys. They guessed passwords. They tried to piece together a person's life from traces and fragments, all while their minds were foggy and their hearts were raw.

Traditional planning was not ineffective because people didn't care. It was ineffective because the tools were not built for real life. They required too much time, too much expertise, too many separate steps, and too much emotional energy. When planning feels intimidating, most people do what humans naturally do with intimidating things: They postpone it.

Technology has transformed what is possible. Modern planning can now take advantage of tools previous generations never had: secure digital storage, encrypted account management, unified platforms that gather everything in one place, and systems that allow plans to be updated as life changes. It can include automated document creation, guided workflows, and even voice or video legacy features that preserve a person's presence in a way paper never could. Technology offers structure. It offers simplicity. It offers accessibility for families who need information quickly. It offers security that protects sensitive details. The modern path uses technology not to replace humanity, but to support it.

Just as important, modern planning focuses on the whole person. Traditional planning centered legal and financial documents, as if those were the only things that mattered. But people are not only legal entities and bank accounts; people are emotional beings with memories, relationships, preferences, values, and stories. The modern path recognizes that end-of-life planning should honor the full story of a life.

That means planning today can include personal wishes, ceremony preferences, legacy messages, practical instructions, contact lists, and emotional guidance. It can include digital accounts and online identities alongside the documents families have always needed. It can help someone express not only what they want done, but who they are and how they want to be remembered. The modern approach respects both the practical and the personal, because families need both.

Accessibility and simplicity are essential in this new era. In the past, planning often felt like a complicated process reserved for people who had the time, money, and confidence to navigate legal systems and appointments. Many people avoided planning not because they didn't understand its importance but because it felt inaccessible. The modern path changes that by prioritizing clarity of language and ease of action. It uses guided questions instead of complicated forms. It uses straightforward, fill-in-the-blank structures that help people begin without fear. It allows plans to be updated easily as life evolves. It removes intimidation, and when intimidation is removed, more people are willing to act. Simplicity opens the door for everyone to plan.

The modern approach also integrates compassion, because planning is not only logistical. It is emotional. It carries weight. It can bring up memories. It can trigger fear. It can require reflection that people have been avoiding for years. A compassionate approach guides gently rather than pushing. It supports rather than overwhelms. It reassures rather than intimidates. Compassion creates emotional safety, allowing people to approach the subject at their own pace. It turns planning into a caring act rather than a chore, and it helps people feel that preparation is something they can do with steadiness, not something they must survive with dread.

Modern planning also recognizes something traditional planning often ignored: it works best when it is shared. Planning should not exist in isolation. Families benefit when conversations open early, when wishes are discussed openly, and when loved ones understand one another's values and preferences. Shared planning reduces confusion and strengthens relationships. It creates transparency that will matter greatly during moments of loss. When people understand one another clearly, they can support one another with unity instead of guessing in silence. Modern planning makes communication part of preparation, not an optional extra.

Because the digital world has become inseparable from modern life, digital organization and security are no longer optional. People have countless digital identities: email accounts, subscriptions, social media profiles, financial apps, online banking, cloud storage. Without organization, families can spend months trying to locate or access these accounts after a loss, often running into barriers that protect privacy but complicate responsibility. Modern planning provides secure tools that gather essential information in one protected place, using encryption for privacy and structure for organization. It creates a secure access system so loved ones can retrieve what they need without unnecessary stress. Digital life must be planned for because digital life is real life now.

Modern planning also supports more than families. It supports employers and workplaces too. Loss doesn't stop at the front door of a home. It follows people into their jobs, their responsibilities, and their daily functioning. Employees dealing with grief and unplanned responsibilities often struggle with focus, productivity, and emotional stability. Employers feel this impact through missed work, increased stress, and disruption. A modern planning model reduces the burden on employees by giving them tools that create clarity, decrease the stress of unexpected responsibilities, and support mental well-being. In doing so, it helps create healthier families and healthier workplaces.

At the heart of all of this is the emotional value of being prepared. Preparedness brings calm, confidence, and peace. People who complete their planning often describe feeling lighter and more grounded. They know they created order.

They know they took responsibility. They know they reduced the emotional burden on the people they love. The value of preparation extends far beyond logistics. It reduces anxiety. It strengthens relationships. It becomes part of a person's internal landscape. Preparedness is emotional stability in action.

Modern planning gives meaning to the future. It is not about anticipating death. It is about honoring life. It is about protecting the people who matter. It is about shaping a story intentionally, not leaving it to chance. Modern planning allows people to leave more than memories. It allows them to leave clarity, connection, guidance, and stability. It allows them to create peace for the people they love. Preparation becomes purpose.

The modern path matters now more than ever because modern life requires it. Today's families are more emotionally complex. Financial lives are more intricate. Digital footprints are larger. Responsibilities stretch across more areas than previous generations could have imagined. Without thoughtful planning, the burdens placed on loved ones can become overwhelming. The modern path exists because the old ways were not enough. It offers clarity in a world full of complexity. It provides tools that match real life. It brings compassionate structure to both emotional and practical needs. The modern path matters because clarity matters.

When people adopt this modern approach, they build a future on intention. They think about legacy. They protect their families. They create meaning in their final chapter. They build a foundation of clarity that outlasts them. This intention becomes an expression of love. It reduces suffering. It strengthens unity. It brings peace where chaos might otherwise appear. The modern path to end-of-life planning is not simply a method; it is a philosophy of living wisely and leaving well.

Chapter 20

How IMTA Reduces Stress for Families and Employers

Families today face overwhelming emotional and logistical burdens when a loved one dies. There is confusion. There are unanswered questions. Documents are missing. Financial details are unclear. Digital accounts are scattered everywhere. At the same time, employers face their own challenges when an employee is suddenly pulled into loss. Productivity drops. Absences rise. Emotional exhaustion ripples through teams.

I Made the Arrangements (*IMTA*) was created for these real-life problems. It was built to replace fear with clarity and chaos with direction. It supports families long before a loss occurs, and it gives employers a meaningful resource that protects the emotional well-being of the people who keep their organizations running. *IMTA* exists because the traditional system leaves too much stress on the people least prepared to carry it. *IMTA* is the bridge between preparation and peace.

The experience is intentionally simple, because simplicity is what makes planning possible. When families use *IMTA*, they are not met with overwhelming forms or intimidating legal language. They are guided through questions written in a way that feels natural and human. They can move at their own pace. They can take one step at a time, and instead of the planning taking months, the process becomes something people can actually complete.

That simplicity matters because planning should not be a struggle. *IMTA* helps families map funeral preferences, create a will, build an advance directive, and store essential information in one organized place. When the time comes, loved ones do not have to search through drawers or dig through files. They do not have to guess. They can open the account and follow the plan. A simple process now becomes profound relief later.

The moment a loss occurs, families need clarity more than anything. *IMTA* provides it—the funeral plan, the will, the advance directive, personal messages, account information, contacts, instructions. The pieces that normally create emotional overload are gathered in a single, accessible place. That organization changes everything. Loved ones feel supported rather than lost. They make decisions confidently rather than fearfully. They honor wishes instead of trying to interpret silence. The emotional difference cannot be overstated. *IMTA* gives families direction during the hardest days of their lives.

This clarity also creates something grief rarely offers on its own: confidence. Uncertainty is one of the most painful parts of loss. People worry they made the wrong choice. They worry they disappointed the person. They worry they failed to honor what mattered. *IMTA* reduces that uncertainty by making wishes clear long before they are needed. When families see the plan in the person's own words, reassurance replaces doubt. Confidence replaces guilt. Grief becomes less complicated because it is not tangled in unanswered questions. Clarity becomes emotional protection.

IMTA supports employers by supporting employees. Loss affects an employee's concentration, productivity, stability, and ability to stay engaged. Most employers want to help, but they are not equipped to manage the emotional and logistical aftershocks of grief. *IMTA* offers a proactive approach. When employees have access to the platform, they can prepare long before they face a loss. That preparation reduces strain when the moment arrives. It shortens the period of confusion. It gives employees structure and direction so they can return to steadiness more quickly. Employers benefit because the workforce is supported rather than overwhelmed.

Workplace stability is not only affected by grief. It is affected by chaos. When an employee experiences a loss without preparation, the ripple effect spreads across a team—projects stall, deadlines shift, coworkers absorb additional responsibilities. Emotional strain moves through the department. Much of that disruption is not caused by grief itself, but by the crisis management that comes from not having a plan. *IMTA* helps protect employers from this instability. Employees who have prepared are not thrown into logistical panic when a family member dies. They know what needs to be done. They have the documents. They have accounts organized. They have direction. That clarity supports steadiness, and steadiness supports the workplace. A prepared employee is a supported employee. A supported employee strengthens the entire organization.

IMTA also reduces the financial and administrative burden that often stretches loss into months of unresolved stress: funeral costs, legal fees, endless tasks, accounts left open, services continuing to bill, creditors stepping in. When families are unprepared, these issues consume time and energy, and employers often see prolonged absences while employees try to sort through unfinished business. *IMTA* alleviates these pressures by helping people organize in advance. Accounts are documented. Services can be canceled with clear instructions. Insurance decisions are easier to navigate. A will can reduce disputes. When the burden is lighter, employees return sooner and with clearer focus.

Mental health is another essential part of the equation. Grief strains emotional health, but uncertainty and responsibility can make that strain debilitating. Employees without a plan often feel overwhelmed by fear, confusion, and pressure. *IMTA* supports mental health by removing uncertainty and restoring a sense of control during a time that feels uncontrollable. It reassures people they have already protected their families. It gives them permission to focus on healing rather than scrambling. Mental health improves when stress decreases, and *IMTA* makes that decrease possible.

IMTA also gives human resources teams a clear structure to point to. HR professionals often carry the responsibility of guiding employees through life's hardest moments, but without a system, they can offer sympathy without real solutions. *IMTA* becomes a tangible resource that empowers employees and reduces strain. It allows HR to introduce proactive planning as part of wellness, to explain why it matters, and to support employees in building clarity long before a crisis occurs. This shifts HR from a reactive support system to a proactive one. Clear systems make compassionate workplaces stronger.

On the family side, *IMTA* helps protect unity. A lack of preparation often leads to conflict: disagreements about funeral choices, finances, responsibilities, and meaning. Employers see the effects when employees become emotionally overwhelmed by family disputes, and that stress can last for months. *IMTA* prevents many of these conflicts by providing one clear source of truth. Everyone sees the plan. Everyone understands the wishes. Everyone knows the intentions. That unity reduces emotional distress and helps employees remain more grounded. Family unity supports healing and workplace stability.

This is why *IMTA* fits naturally into modern wellness programs. Many workplace wellness strategies focus on physical and mental health, but rarely address one of the most significant events employees will face. Loss is universal. It affects emotional well-being, productivity, and long-term mental health. *IMTA* fills that gap. It supports employees in a way that feels human and meaningful. It strengthens an employer's commitment to compassion. A modern wellness program recognizes that life includes loss and prepares people for it.

Employees who complete planning often describe an emotional lightness. They feel prepared. They feel responsible. They feel relieved. They know they removed future burdens from the people they love. They know that when loss occurs, the practical side of life will not collapse. That relief affects daily life too. It reduces anxiety. It improves focus. It fosters calm thinking. It builds resilience. Employers benefit because prepared employees are less distracted and more emotionally stable. Preparation does not only protect the future. It enriches the present.

IMTA matters because life is fast, responsibilities are heavy, families are stretched, and workplaces are demanding. In that environment, uncertainty becomes chronic stress. *IMTA* provides clarity where people expect chaos. It offers structure where people anticipate confusion. It brings peace where stress normally takes over. And that clarity is not only useful during loss. It changes how people move through the world. It encourages responsibility. It strengthens relationships. It protects emotional wellness. *IMTA* is not just a planning platform; it is a stabilizing force.

The future of end-of-life preparation will emphasize humanity over fear, clarity over confusion, and connection over avoidance. *IMTA* embodies that shift. It offers families and employers a pathway that matches modern emotional and practical needs. This is not about preparing for death. It is about living wisely. It is about reducing suffering that comes from uncertainty. It is about honoring the people who matter most by easing the burdens they will one day face. *IMTA* is part of a movement toward a more compassionate future where planning becomes an act of love.

Chapter 21

A CULTURE OF PREPARATION AND PEACE

Every generation passes along certain values: responsibility, compassion, courage, integrity. These are the qualities that hold families and communities together. Preparation belongs on that list as well, not as an administrative detail but as a fundamental act of care. Preparation is how we protect the people who will one day carry the weight of our absence. It is how we show love in a way that lasts.

For too long, planning for the end of life has been treated as optional, uncomfortable, or something to postpone until it becomes unavoidable. People act as though preparation is morbid, as if naming reality somehow invites it. But every person eventually reaches the same moment of transition. Preparation is not morbid. It is mature. It is human. It is a gift that ensures the people we love will face less stress in one of the hardest moments of their lives. A culture of preparation begins when people recognize that clarity is an expression of love.

Avoidance, however, has shaped the way most families approach this subject. People shy away because it feels heavy. They assume bringing it up will create anxiety. They hope ignoring it will protect loved ones from discomfort. But avoidance does not protect. It transfers responsibility. It creates silence where clarity should exist.

The cost of that silence arrives later. Families face difficult decisions with no guidance. They guess instead of knowing. They carry doubt where reassurance was needed. They enter grief already burdened, not only by loss but by uncertainty. Avoidance creates unnecessary emotional weight during an already fragile time. Breaking this cycle requires a cultural shift. It requires people to view planning as a normal part of life rather than an uncomfortable exception.

One of the most powerful ways to shift a culture is to change what we treat as a milestone. Many important tasks in life follow predictable patterns. People create financial plans. They save for retirement. They purchase insurance. They prepare for weddings, births, and career changes. These milestones are embraced because they represent responsibility and stability.

End-of-life planning deserves the same level of acceptance. It is not a separate category. It belongs within the continuum of life. When society treats planning as expected, people approach it with less fear and more confidence. They begin to see it as a natural step that ensures their story is finished with intention. Making planning a milestone shifts the emotional tone from fear to empowerment.

Families who talk openly about preparation discover a different kind of strength. Conversations that once felt scary become opportunities for connection. People learn about one another's values. They understand preferences. They clarify responsibilities. They remove the possibility of conflict before it ever has a chance to appear. These conversations reduce anxiety because they replace imagination with reality, and reality is usually more manageable than the fear people carry in silence. Open conversations build trust between generations. They help families approach life's challenges as a team rather than as isolated individuals. A culture of preparation grows stronger when communication becomes natural and compassionate.

Education plays a central role in changing cultural norms. Many people avoid planning because they do not understand it. They assume it is complex. They assume it requires legal knowledge. They assume it must be expensive. These misunderstandings keep people stuck, even when they want to do the right thing.

Education changes the emotional landscape. When people learn that planning can be simple and accessible, they feel empowered to begin. When they understand that preparation reduces stress and strengthens families, they become more open to it. When they see tools that make it easier, they feel relief. Education breaks down fear and builds a culture of readiness, because clarity becomes something people can actually reach.

One of the most important shifts is normalizing planning through everyday life. People already make thoughtful decisions daily. They prepare meals. They plan trips. They schedule appointments. They manage finances. When planning becomes part of that normal rhythm, it stops feeling like a distant obligation and starts feeling like a familiar expression of responsibility.

Normalizing planning means integrating it slowly and gently. One task at a time. One conversation at a time. One thoughtful choice at a time. Over time, people begin to see preparation as ordinary. And when planning becomes ordinary, it becomes far less intimidating.

Shared responsibility strengthens family bonds as well. When a family understands the plan, each person carries a piece of responsibility. No one feels alone. No one feels overwhelmed. No one feels confused. This shared preparation builds emotional closeness because it builds trust. Families learn how each member thinks. They understand what matters to each person. They develop a sense of unity that becomes invaluable when life gets hard. A culture of preparation strengthens the emotional foundation of the family.

It also reduces intergenerational stress. One of the greatest gifts preparation provides is that it prevents avoidable strain from being passed down. When older generations prepare, they protect their children from confusion and emotional overload. When younger generations observe that preparation, they learn from it. They adopt it. They carry those habits into their own lives. Over time, stress decreases across generations because clarity becomes part of the inheritance. Intergenerational clarity becomes a form of emotional stability passed through time.

Planning can even help people live with greater purpose. When people confront the reality that time is finite, they often become more intentional. They focus on what truly matters. They strengthen relationships. They prioritize meaningful experiences. They live with deeper gratitude. Planning does not diminish life; it elevates it. It encourages reflection on values and alignment between daily choices and what someone believes matters most. Preparation inspires a more purposeful life.

For many, preparation brings a peace they did not expect. Every person has the ability to reduce the burden their loved ones will one day face. When someone completes planning, the relief can be surprising. People describe feeling calm, grounded, and ready. They know they have done their part. That peace becomes part of their emotional landscape. It influences relationships. It strengthens responsibility. It allows people to move forward with confidence rather than fear. Preparation becomes a lasting source of inner peace.

Communities also play a vital role in shaping this culture. Faith leaders, educators, wellness professionals, employers, and trusted advisors influence cultural attitudes. When these figures normalize planning, entire groups begin to embrace preparation as an act of love. Workplaces can help by offering tools and resources that make planning easier and less isolating. When people see planning valued in the spaces where they spend their lives, they feel safer participating. A culture grows strongest when supported by both families and communities.

Changing the narrative around planning is essential. For generations, planning has been associated with fear, discomfort, and avoidance. A healthier narrative recognizes the truth: Planning is not about expecting death. It is about protecting life. It is about caring for the people who will remain. It is about giving clarity instead of leaving chaos. When that narrative shifts, people feel empowered instead of overwhelmed. They feel peace instead of fear. A new narrative creates a new emotional landscape.

A culture of peace matters now more than ever. Society is faster, more digital, and more complex. Families need stability. Workplaces need structure. Individuals need tools that protect emotional well-being. A culture of preparation reduces suffering that never needed to exist. It strengthens relationships. It creates unity. It promotes emotional health. It builds a foundation for future generations who will benefit from the clarity left behind. A culture of peace becomes a gift passed down through time.

The path forward begins the way all cultural change begins: with small steps. One person choosing clarity. One family beginning a conversation. One employer offering meaningful tools. One community leader encouraging responsibility. Each step brings us closer to a culture defined by peace rather than fear.

When people choose preparation, they choose compassion. They choose clarity. They choose connection. They choose love expressed through thoughtful action. This is how a culture of preparation grows. This is how peace takes root. A culture of preparation is ultimately a culture of love.

Chapter 22

WHAT IT MEANS TO LEAVE A LEGACY OF CLARITY

Many people assume legacy is formed only by what remains in memory. The stories that get repeated. The photographs that get passed around. The traditions that keep showing up year after year. Those things matter deeply, but they are only part of the picture. A true legacy is also defined by the clarity a person gives to the people they love. Clarity shapes emotional experience. It shapes relationships. It shapes the way grief unfolds.

A legacy of clarity becomes a gift that lasts longer than any possession. It reduces confusion. It prevents conflict. It provides direction during the heaviest days. It creates peace in a moment when many families experience fear and uncertainty. Memories alone cannot do that. Clarity can, and when someone leaves clarity behind, what they are really leaving is love expressed in a form that can be used.

Without clear wishes, families are forced into guesswork. They try to interpret what the person might have wanted. They search their memories for clues. They replay conversations, hoping a casual remark can function as instruction. They hope they are choosing correctly, because the fear of choosing wrong feels like the fear of letting someone down. Guesswork becomes emotional weight that lingers long after the loss. Even when decisions were made with good intentions, uncertainty keeps a question alive in the mind: *Was this what they would have wanted?*

Clarity removes that burden. It lifts the strain that uncertainty creates. It gives loved ones confidence instead of fear. It allows them to feel connected to the person's intentions rather than distant from them. Guesswork adds stress to grief. Clarity lifts that stress away.

When someone leaves behind detailed wishes, their guidance becomes a source of comfort. Families feel supported even though the person is no longer physically present. They feel guided. They feel reassured. They feel anchored by the knowledge that they are honoring the person correctly. Definitive guidance brings steadiness. It helps loved ones move through early grief with clearer minds. They know what needs to be done. They know how to proceed. They do not feel lost, and they do not feel overwhelmed by choices they never wanted to make under pressure. Their sorrow is real, but it is no longer buried beneath layers of confusion. Guidance becomes a calming presence that continues long after life has ended.

Clarity also strengthens family unity. Conflict after a loss is more common than most families expect. Emotions are heightened. Grief expresses itself differently in different people. Disagreements arise when no plan exists, and even small decisions can become sources of tension. In grief, every detail can feel symbolic, and every difference of opinion can feel personal.

Clarity protects families from these conflicts. When wishes are fully expressed, there is a single source of truth to follow. No one has to interpret. No one has to compete for authority. The family can focus on honoring the person and supporting one another. Clarity strengthens unity at a time when unity matters most.

A legacy of clarity also reduces long-term regret. Regret can attach itself to grief and stay for years. People question choices long after the loss. They replay moments again and again, searching for reassurance that never comes. They wonder if the person would have approved. They wonder if they missed something important. That uncertainty can become a permanent companion.

Clarity removes the conditions where that regret grows. Loved ones know exactly what was wanted. They can follow those wishes with confidence. Their grief does not become entangled with second-guessing. In that way, clarity becomes emotional protection long after the loss has passed.

Clarity also gives loved ones something grief rarely offers on its own: space. Healing requires time and mental freedom. When families are forced to solve logistical problems during grief, they lose the room they need to mourn. Their attention stays divided. Their nervous systems stay in crisis mode. Their hearts do not get to be hearts, because their minds are being asked to act like administrators.

Clarity creates room for healing. When practical decisions have already been made, loved ones can focus on emotional needs. They can sit with their grief without being pulled into a maze of paperwork and urgent choices. They can lean on one another instead of being scattered by stress. A legacy of clarity gives people the freedom to heal.

Clarity also honors a life authentically. Wishes represent identity. Beliefs. Meaning. The vision someone had for how their life should be honored. When those wishes are followed, the farewell becomes a reflection of who the person truly was. The story is told truthfully. Values remain visible even in the final chapter.

Families often feel grateful when they can honor those wishes. They feel they are completing the person's final chapter with dignity. They feel connected through the act of honoring a voice that was expressed in advance. That authenticity brings both comfort and pride. A legacy of clarity ensures that the final expression of a life remains faithful to the person who lived it.

Clarity also bridges emotional distance between generations. Children and grandchildren do not always know the deeper priorities of the older generation. Without clarity, younger generations can miss the chance to understand a person's worldview, values, and reasoning. That gap can create distance, even inside loving families.

A legacy of clarity changes that. It reveals priorities. It explains preferences. It gives future generations insight into the emotional and philosophical foundations of the person's life. In that way, clarity becomes a story passed from one generation to the next, strengthening family identity across time.

Loss interrupts life. It disrupts routines. It breaks patterns. It leaves people unsteady. Clarity creates continuity in the middle of that disruption. Loved ones know what happens next. They have instructions that provide structure to the days and weeks after the loss. That structure brings rhythm to a time that might otherwise feel chaotic. It helps grieving families feel grounded. Clarity softens disruption by giving families a path to follow.

A legacy of clarity extends beyond the practical. Many people think planning is only documents and directions, but clarity reaches deeper than logistics. It shapes emotional well-being. It strengthens relationships. It influences how families remember the person and how they move through their own lives afterward. A legacy of clarity becomes part of a family's emotional fabric. It teaches responsibility. It teaches compassion. It teaches that preparing for the sake of others is a form of love. It encourages future generations to build clarity into their own lives. A legacy of clarity becomes a generational gift.

Clarity also reduces fear about death itself. Fear often grows from the unknown. When people do not prepare, they fear uncertainty. They fear the pressures they might leave behind.

They fear what their loved ones might face. That fear can linger for years, quietly shaping the way someone lives.

Creating clarity softens that fear. It relieves the mind because responsibility has been taken. It eases the emotional load on the family. It replaces uncertainty with understanding. Mortality becomes calmer, more grounded, less shadowed by panic. Clarity brings structure to what otherwise feels like the unknown.

Leaving clarity, ultimately, is a lasting act of love. When everything is stripped away, what remains is love expressed through choices, responsibilities, and protection. Leaving clarity says the following:

I want to protect you.

I want to make this easier for you.

I want you to have peace.

I want you to remember me without confusion or conflict.

I want to leave calm instead of chaos.

Clarity transforms planning into love expressed through action.

This is often what future generations remember most. They remember the stories and the laughter. They remember the lessons and the values. But they also remember how they felt in the first days and weeks after the loss. They remember whether they were overwhelmed or supported, lost or guided. When clarity exists, those memories are gentler. The transition is smoother. The emotional wounds are fewer. The legacy becomes one of thoughtfulness, care, and protection. That kind of legacy does not fade.

A well-planned life extends beyond accomplishments. It includes the responsibility someone takes to ensure their final chapter reflects intention. A life that ends with clarity leaves behind meaning that supports the people who remain. It becomes a reminder that preparation matters. It becomes part of family identity. It becomes a symbol of love carried into the future.

A legacy of clarity is not only about how someone is remembered. It is about how they continue to guide and protect the people they love long after they are gone.

Chapter 23

THE EMOTIONAL IMPACT
OF LEAVING ORDER
INSTEAD OF CHAOS

When someone dies without leaving structure behind, the people who love them are forced into a whirlwind at the very moment their hearts are breaking. Shock and sorrow collide with paperwork, phone calls, and urgent decisions. People search through drawers. They look for documents they are not even sure exist. They try to understand financial obligations that were never discussed. They attempt to make choices with limited information while their minds are already struggling to hold the reality of the loss.

That disorder does more than create stress. It intensifies grief. It forces people into crisis mode when they are emotionally fragile. It adds confusion on top of heartbreak. It deepens exhaustion. It steals time that should belong to mourning. Chaos becomes an emotional weight that delays healing, because the nervous system cannot fully grieve when it is still trying to survive the logistics. Order, then, is not simply organization; it is protection. It shields the grieving heart from unnecessary suffering.

When a plan exists, the early days of grief feel different. There is still sorrow. There is still pain. But there is direction. Loved ones know where to begin. They know what the person wanted. They know what steps to take. They are not forced to improvise while their emotions are raw and unsteady. Structure gives grief a gentler shape. It allows families to move through tasks with steadiness instead of fear. It creates a sense of safety in an otherwise disorienting moment.

There is something else that happens when order exists: Even though the person who made the plan is no longer physically present, their foresight becomes a presence. The plan feels like a guiding hand in the room. It brings calm not because it removes sadness, but because it removes uncertainty. In that way, order becomes emotional protection.

Order also reduces family tension before it begins. Emotions run high during loss, and stress makes communication fragile. Even close families struggle when there is no guidance. People remember different conversations. They interpret remarks differently. They carry different emotional needs and different beliefs about what is respectful. Those differences become disagreements. Disagreements become arguments. Arguments can become lasting damage.

A well-prepared plan prevents these fractures. Loved ones follow the same instructions. They honor the same decisions. They share the same understanding. This shared direction makes conflict far less likely to take root. Families that might have fractured under pressure stay connected, because the person they lost gave them stability when they needed it most. Order preserves unity.

One of the most painful parts of loss is the feeling of not knowing what to do: Not knowing what service the person wanted. Not knowing what financial obligations exist. Not knowing which account needs to be closed. Not knowing who should be notified. Not knowing what message the person hoped to leave behind. This uncertainty feels like walking through fog. Every step is uncertain. Every decision feels risky. People fear disappointing the person who is gone. They fear upsetting family members. They fear choosing incorrectly. Order removes that fog. It gives direction when direction is needed most.

Order also restores a sense of control when life feels uncontrollable. Loss can make people feel powerless. Something irreversible has happened, and nothing could stop it. That helplessness can be overwhelming. But when a clear plan is in place, loved ones regain footing. They know what is expected. They know how to move forward. They feel capable rather than helpless. This sense of control does not eliminate grief. It makes grief bearable. It gives people the strength to keep functioning, to return to responsibilities with steadier minds, to breathe again. Order gives people the emotional footing they need to stand.

It also protects loved ones from being overwhelmed. In the early days after a death, the smallest task can feel enormous: A phone call. A form. A search for a document. Grief takes so much energy that even simple responsibilities feel heavy. When everything is disorganized, those tasks multiply. People feel buried before they begin. Order reduces that burden by gathering details in one place, answering questions before they arise, and giving loved ones tools so they do not have to build the structure themselves. Instead of drowning, they can move one step at a time with guidance. That protection allows healing to begin earlier, with fewer setbacks.

Order helps people mourn without distraction. Grief is not only emotional. It is physical. The body carries it. The mind slows. Concentration weakens. People need space to mourn. They need freedom to feel without constant interruption. Chaos interrupts that process. Disorganization demands attention when attention should be on the heart. A well-prepared plan gives people breathing room. They can mourn instead of managing a crisis. They can sit with memories. They can support one another. They can process emotion instead of paperwork. Order honors the emotional needs of the grieving.

It also encourages compassion within the family. When everyone understands the plan, people become gentler. They are not debating. They are not scrambling. They are not competing for control. Emotional space opens, and compassion fills it. People comfort one another instead of correcting one another. They become more patient, more understanding, more tender. Order sets the emotional tone in the room. It allows love to take precedence over stress. Compassion grows naturally when the groundwork has already been laid.

The way a loss unfolds becomes part of how a person is remembered. If the experience was chaotic, families may carry negative emotions for years. They may associate the loss with confusion and exhaustion instead of reflection and love. That emotional weight becomes part of the story. Order creates a different memory. Loved ones look back and remember feeling guided. They remember feeling supported. They remember having room to breathe. They remember honoring a life instead of struggling through the aftermath. Order becomes part of the legacy the person leaves behind.

Order also strengthens the healing process because healing depends on stability. When the practical side of loss is organized, people can enter the emotional work of grief with more strength. They do not feel stuck. They do not feel overwhelmed. They do not feel lost. They feel steady enough to face what they feel. That steadiness supports healthier healing patterns. Acceptance arrives more naturally. People regain footing sooner. Emotional setbacks become less severe. Order is not a substitute for healing, but it creates the conditions where healing can unfold.

Order protects family resources too. Chaos is not only emotional. It can be financially damaging. Missing information leads to rushed decisions. Important accounts can be overlooked. Unwanted expenses can pile up. Administrative mistakes can create additional stress. Order protects against these losses by organizing documents, outlining accounts, clarifying responsibilities, identifying insurance, and preventing unnecessary expenses. In that way, order becomes financial stewardship as well as emotional care.

Order offers stability to the most vulnerable members of the family. Children and teenagers experience loss differently from adults. Their understanding is still forming. Emotions can be intense and unpredictable. When the adults around them are overwhelmed, younger family members feel even more insecure. They internalize tension. They feel unsafe when the world suddenly has no structure. Order provides emotional safety. When adults have direction, they can communicate more clearly, maintain routines, and approach the loss with steadiness. That steadiness becomes a stabilizing force for young people who rely on adults to guide them through unfamiliar grief. Order becomes protection.

Order also helps loved ones maintain dignity. Grief can make people feel exposed. They fear making mistakes. They fear being judged. They fear appearing weak. When everything is disorganized, those fears intensify. People may feel embarrassed that they cannot find documents or answer basic questions. They may feel overwhelmed when asked for information they do not have. Order preserves dignity. Loved ones can respond with confidence. They can carry out responsibilities with calmness. They feel capable rather than confused. That dignity supports self-esteem during one of the most vulnerable periods of life. Order becomes a gift of respect.

In the end, leaving order instead of chaos is a final expression of love. When someone prepares thoughtfully, they are doing more than organizing documents. They are creating emotional shelter for the people who will one day stand in their absence. They are easing pain. They are preventing conflict. They are giving direction. They are protecting the people they love from stress they should never have to endure.

Leaving order is a final message that says, "I thought of you. I wanted to make this easier for you. I wanted you to have peace." That message becomes one of the most meaningful parts of a legacy. Order is love expressed through foresight and responsibility.

Chapter 24

WHY PLANNING IS AN ACT OF LOVE

When people think about love, they often picture affection, support, shared memories, celebration, comfort. But one of the deepest expressions of love is responsibility. Love is not only what we feel. It is what we are willing to carry. It is the willingness to protect the people who matter most, even when the work of protection is uncomfortable. Planning for the future, especially for the end of life, is responsibility rooted in love.

Planning says, "I want to take care of you even when I am no longer here to do it in person." It says, "I value your well-being enough to organize what might otherwise overwhelm you." It says, "I want to spare you from confusion and hardship." In that way, planning becomes a quiet but powerful form of devotion. Love is not only the warmth we share. It is also the preparation we leave behind.

One of the hardest truths about life is that loss arrives whether or not we are ready for it. The people we love will one day face that moment. They will carry the emotional weight of grief, and they will step into a world that suddenly feels unfamiliar. In that fragile space, the last thing they should encounter is a maze of decisions and unanswered questions.

Planning lifts that burden. It removes obstacles before they appear. It eases responsibilities that would otherwise land on grieving hearts. It offers the people we love room to breathe, room to mourn, room to remember. That freedom is not small. It is a gift that protects emotional well-being when emotional strength is at its lowest. Love makes life easier for the ones who remain.

A plan is also more than a collection of instructions. It becomes a voice. It becomes a final message that says, "I cared enough to think this through. I cared enough to guide you. I cared enough to leave no confusion." When the world feels unsteady, that guidance feels comforting and familiar. It reminds loved ones of values, personality, thoughtfulness, tenderness. It allows them to "hear" you even in your absence. They feel supported by foresight. They feel connected in a moment that might otherwise feel overwhelming. Planning becomes a continuation of your love story.

Planning also protects family unity. Loss can test even strong families. Emotions run high. People interpret things differently. Grief amplifies tension. Without direction, disagreements can appear quickly and painfully. Those fractures can create emotional wounds that last far beyond the funeral.

Planning prevents much of this. It removes uncertainty, which is often the true fuel of conflict. When wishes are clear, everyone has the same reference point. Everyone understands what should happen. Everyone follows one clear message rather than relying on assumptions, partial memories, or competing interpretations. Unity becomes a shield that protects relationships from unnecessary strain. Love protects families from fracture.

Planning also respects the emotional weight of grief. Grief demands energy, focus, and emotional strength. When people must manage endless decisions at the same time, they feel stretched beyond their limits. Planning acknowledges this emotional reality and responds with compassion. It reduces the load grieving people have to carry. It allows them to focus on healing rather than scrambling. This respect for their emotional experience is one of the most meaningful forms of love, because it is empathy that reaches beyond your own life and into theirs. Love respects the emotional journey as much as the practical one.

Dignity is another gift preparation protects. When wishes are known and documented, loved ones do not have to make uncomfortable decisions on someone else's behalf. They do not have to guess. They do not have to choose between possibilities that may or may not reflect the person's values. A clear plan protects dignity by ensuring the final chapter is handled with intention and respect. It reassures loved ones that they are honoring you exactly as you hoped. It protects them from the fear of making a mistake, and it preserves the integrity of your story. Love honors dignity until the very end.

Planning also protects the young and the vulnerable. Children and teenagers feel the ripple of loss in intense ways, and their sense of safety depends on the stability around them. When adults are overwhelmed by logistical chaos, young people feel anxious and unsteady. When adults have direction, young people feel sheltered. Planning strengthens that emotional safety. It gives caregivers structure. It reduces stress in the home. It prevents turbulence from being passed down to the youngest members of the family. Preparation becomes a shield. Love shelters those who look to us for stability.

Thinking ahead also invites honest conversations, and those conversations are themselves acts of love. They may feel difficult at first, unfamiliar, even awkward. But once they begin, they often open the door to deeper connection. Families learn one another more clearly. They discuss hopes and values. They explore the meaning of life and the legacy they want to leave. These conversations bring people closer. They strengthen trust. They reduce misunderstandings. They deepen emotional connection. In many families, they become some of the most important conversations they ever have. Love grows in honest dialogue.

Planning can also include legacy messages: letters, videos, words of wisdom, gratitude, reflections. These become treasures. They help loved ones feel presence long after you are gone. They offer comfort during hard moments. They become emotional keepsakes that support healing. When planning includes thoughtful messages, your voice continues to guide and comfort. Loved ones are reminded of character, values, and affection. Those words can shape memory for decades. Love continues through words that endure beyond a lifetime.

The influence of planning doesn't stop with one generation. A thoughtful plan benefits immediate family, but it also teaches future generations. Children who witness responsible planning grow up understanding its importance. They learn that preparedness is part of loving others. They adopt the habits and pass them on. Over time, this creates a lineage of responsibility and compassion and reduces emotional burden for generations not yet born. Love extends forward in time when responsibility is taught by example.

In the earliest days after a loss, when emotions are fragile, a plan can bring a calm atmosphere. Loved ones know what to do. They know they are fulfilling wishes. They move with purpose rather than fear. Peace softens the edges of grief. Preparation provides reassurance that lingers in the heart long after the initial shock has passed. Loved ones remember that choices were made with their well-being in mind. Love offers peace even when you are no longer there to speak it.

Planning also reduces regret for those who remain. Regret is one of the most painful emotions after loss. People wonder if they made the right choices, if they honored the person correctly, if they forgot something important. That struggle can last for years. A thoughtful plan removes the conditions that create regret. Loved ones know what was wanted. They follow instructions with confidence. They carry out the story in a way that feels authentic. Instead of regret, they feel gratitude. Love removes the weight regret so often leaves behind.

Ultimately, planning fulfills a final responsibility we all share. Every person reaches the moment when loved ones must navigate life without them. Planning acknowledges this reality with courage and compassion. It affirms that caring for others does not end when life ends. It continues through the order and guidance we leave behind. This fulfillment becomes a final expression of character, a gesture that says, "I lived with intention, and I leave with intention." Love fulfills responsibility all the way to the final moment.

When all the pieces come together, planning reveals its true nature. It is not merely a legal task. It is not a formality. It is love made visible. It is devotion translated into structure. It is care expressed through preparation. It is gratitude for the people who shaped your life and protection for the people who will carry your memory forward. Planning turns love into something tangible that others can lean on when the world feels heavy. Love prepares. Love protects. Love leaves order where chaos would otherwise take root.

Chapter 25

STRENGTHENING THE HUMAN SPIRIT THROUGH PREPAREDNESS

There are certain choices in life that strengthen a person from the inside out, and preparedness is one of them. When someone takes the time to organize their affairs, something subtle but unmistakable begins to change. They feel steadier. More grounded. More capable. They feel a deeper sense of command over the life they are living, not because life becomes predictable but because they have chosen to meet life with intention.

This confidence is not loud. It is not boastful. It does not try to impress anyone. It is quiet and steady, the kind of confidence that comes from knowing important things are not being avoided or left to chance. In a world that can shift without warning, preparedness creates a sense of control that is real, not imagined. Knowing your affairs are in order brings a peace that may be difficult to describe, but easy to recognize in the way it changes how you move through daily life. Preparedness strengthens the spirit by reminding you that you are capable of shaping your future with intention.

Preparedness also acts as an antidote to fear, because much of fear is born from uncertainty. People fear what they cannot predict, what they cannot understand, what they do not feel ready to face. When someone avoids thinking about the later chapters of life, that fear does not disappear. It simply becomes quieter, settling into the background like a constant low hum. It is never loud, but it is always there.

Preparedness eases that hum. When a person organizes plans, they reduce the unknown. They replace uncertainty with structure, and avoidance with understanding. This does not make someone immune to anxiety, but it does build calm that comes from action. Fear loses power when the mind is prepared, because preparation transforms the vague and threatening into something clear and manageable.

Ironically, planning for the future often helps people live more fully in the present. When someone knows important matters are handled, emotional space opens. They feel lighter. They focus more easily on relationships and experiences that matter. They engage more deeply in life because they are no longer weighed down by unfinished responsibility. Preparedness releases a person from the psychological tension that follows them silently when something important is being postponed. When that tension lifts, it makes room for joy. It invites gratitude. It encourages people to pursue goals and passions without the lingering sense that something meaningful has been neglected. Preparedness strengthens the spirit by removing quiet burdens that limit a person's ability to live well.

Preparedness also cultivates emotional resilience. Life is unpredictable. Illness, accidents, sudden loss, unexpected changes—these events test every human being. When someone is unprepared, the shock feels heavier, because there is no foundation to lean on. People feel exposed, as if life has taken the ground from beneath them. Preparedness builds resilience by creating structure before instability arrives. It offers a fallback. It allows someone to respond rather than panic. It does not eliminate pain, but it helps people move through difficult experiences with more strength and clarity. Preparedness becomes a form of emotional training that reinforces the spirit long before adversity appears.

In the process, preparedness encourages a purpose-driven life. When someone sits down to plan, they reflect on values. They consider the meaning of their life. They think about the people they love and how they want to protect them. They examine priorities. Planning becomes an invitation to ask deeper questions: What impact do I want to leave? How do I want to be remembered? What matters most to me? These questions shape daily decisions. They align actions with values. They strengthen integrity and intentionality. Preparedness deepens the spirit by encouraging people to live with purpose rather than habit.

Preparedness also requires emotional honesty. It asks someone to acknowledge that life is finite and to face the reality that loved ones will one day need guidance. These truths are not easy, but confronting them builds maturity. It teaches a person to face reality with grace rather than denial. It encourages humility and kindness in the way they live each day, because it softens the illusion that anything is guaranteed. Preparedness becomes a kind of emotional discipline that shapes the heart as much as it shapes the plan. Honesty with oneself is one of the strongest foundations a person can build.

For many, preparedness also protects personal identity. People worry that in a crisis their values will be forgotten, their voice overlooked, their wishes lost under circumstances. Preparedness protects against that fear by documenting preferences clearly. It preserves autonomy. It preserves story. It ensures that identity remains respected, even when someone cannot speak for themselves. The spirit gains strength from knowing that who you are will not be erased by the chaos of a moment.

Preparedness also builds trust within families. Trust is not created in one conversation. It grows through repeated choices that show reliability and care. When someone prepares, they show loved ones they have thought ahead. They demonstrate care by removing confusion and reducing future stress. They reinforce that love is steady and dependable, not only in emotion but in action. This trust becomes emotional fuel for the family. It strengthens bonds. It encourages communication. It reduces conflict. It creates an atmosphere where vulnerability feels safe. Preparedness strengthens family trust in ways that echo for years.

It also helps people face change with greater grace. Life brings transitions: aging, illness, shifts in family roles, unexpected responsibilities. These changes can feel frightening when someone feels unprepared. But when structures are already in place, people feel more capable. They have already done some of the emotional and practical work that makes transitions less overwhelming. This steadiness is one of the hallmarks of a strong human spirit. Preparedness does not remove uncertainty. It strengthens the person facing it.

That strength spreads outward. When someone is prepared, loved ones often feel more secure. They feel reassured that the future has been considered. They feel relieved knowing they will not be left unprotected. They feel connected through the care that was taken. This emotional security shapes the atmosphere of a home and can ripple through generations, influencing how children learn responsibility and how partners face challenges together. Preparedness creates a foundation of emotional safety for the family.

Preparedness can even reinforce self-worth. Taking responsibility for one's life and choices sends a message inward: My life matters enough to be organized, my relationships matter enough to protect, my story matters enough to shape intentionally. This strengthens identity and creates a deeper sense of personal value. Self-worth grows not only from accomplishments, but from the way a person cares for themselves and others. Preparedness affirms that you are worthy of thoughtful stewardship.

Often, preparedness also encourages more compassionate living. When someone becomes more aware of life's fragility, judgment softens. Patience grows. People listen more deeply. They appreciate relationships more. They recognize that everyone is carrying a story, and that awareness can transform how someone moves through the world. Preparedness strengthens the spirit by deepening empathy and encouraging generosity. It connects the heart to the experiences of others.

Over time, preparedness leaves a legacy of courage. Future generations look back and see someone who faced life honestly, took responsibility, and cared deeply. That example becomes inspiration. It shapes family narrative. It encourages children and grandchildren to build strong lives through intention and preparation. Preparedness leaves behind a story of strength.

Then, finally, preparedness becomes a gift to the spirit itself. It benefits loved ones, but it also benefits the person who prepares. It cultivates peace. It reinforces identity. It deepens meaning. It strengthens resilience. It relieves internal tension. It allows someone to live more fully, knowing nothing important has been ignored. Preparedness honors life, honors relationships, and honors the personal journey. A well-prepared spirit is a strong spirit.

Chapter 26

REFRAMING DEATH AS PART OF A WELL-LIVED LIFE

Most people grow up thinking of death as something separate from life. Something dark. Something distant. Something that sits at the far edge of existence, best ignored until the last possible moment. But death is not an intruder that suddenly appears out of nowhere. It is woven into the same fabric as birth, growth, connection, and change. It is part of the same journey.

When someone begins to see death this way, it stops feeling like a frightening interruption and starts to feel like a natural companion. Not a threat that arrives later, but a truth that has walked alongside every breath, every season, every turning point. This understanding softens fear. It allows people to hold life with more appreciation. It brings depth to moments that might otherwise go unnoticed. Reframing death does not diminish life. It enriches it.

One reason death remains so heavy is the stigma around talking about it. In many cultures it is treated like a forbidden topic. People whisper. They avoid the subject. They behave as though speaking about death invites it closer. But silence does not protect anyone. It isolates people from the emotional and practical tools that make loss more bearable. It keeps families unprepared and alone in the moments when they most need connection.

When people are willing to talk about death with openness and honesty, something powerful happens. Fear loosens its grip. Knowledge grows. Empathy expands. Families learn more about one another's wishes and values. People begin making choices based on intention instead of avoidance. Conversation becomes one of the most effective ways to reframe death as a natural part of life, because what is spoken becomes less frightening than what is hidden.

Awareness of mortality also deepens gratitude. People often say life feels more precious after a close call or a loss. Days feel sharper. Relationships feel richer. Gratitude rises. That shift happens because mortality creates clarity. It reminds people that time has weight and meaning. But we do not have to wait for crisis to access that depth.

When someone embraces awareness before pain forces it upon them, they gain the same richness without the same shock. They notice details more readily. They express appreciation more often. They stop postponing important conversations. They become more conscious of the fact that time with loved ones is not infinite. Awareness of death, held gently, can inspire a fuller appreciation for life.

Reframing death also encourages intentional living. When a person accepts that life has an endpoint, choices begin to change. People think more carefully about how they spend their time. They consider how they want to be remembered. They focus on relationships that nourish them and loosen their grip on relationships that drain them. They pursue goals that reflect their values rather than pressure from the outside world.

Intention sharpens priorities. It ignites creativity. It strengthens commitment to growth. It teaches people to choose meaning over distraction. A life lived with intention is one of the greatest gifts someone can give themselves, and the awareness of mortality is often what makes intention feel urgent enough to act on.

This awareness also helps people accept what they cannot control. Human beings spend an enormous amount of energy trying to control outcomes. They want predictable paths. They want certainty. They want reassurance that life will unfold exactly as imagined. But life rarely follows a script. Change is constant. Loss is inevitable. Control is limited.

When death is reframed as natural, people stop fighting what is unavoidable. Acceptance reduces anxiety because it frees the mind from the exhausting need to pretend that everything can be managed. It creates space for peace. It encourages people to focus on what they can influence: choices, relationships, character, the way they show up for others. Acceptance frees the mind from tension that would otherwise linger for years.

In a deeper sense, death gives life its shape. Life without an endpoint would feel strangely empty. Purpose would lose urgency. Decisions would lose meaning. Relationships could drift endlessly without depth. It is the finiteness of life that gives weight to commitments and urgency to love. It is mortality that teaches people to treat time as precious instead of expendable.

When people begin to see death not as an enemy, but as a defining boundary, they often appreciate the architecture of their lives more clearly. They see how each relationship and each choice forms an arc. They recognize beauty in every season of living, including the seasons that once felt uncomfortable to name.

Looking outward can help too. Many cultures around the world approach death with openness and reverence. Some celebrate life through colorful festivals. Some keep memories alive through rituals that honor ancestors. Some talk openly about mortality at young ages so the subject carries less fear. In many places, death is seen as a continuation of community, not the end of connection.

These perspectives offer insight: Fear of death is not universal. It is learned, and what is learned can be reshaped. When people adopt even a small part of these approaches, they often find themselves more at ease with life's ending. Reframing death sometimes begins simply by noticing that others have already learned how to hold it with less panic and more peace.

Accepting mortality also encourages emotional maturity. Emotional maturity grows when people face truths others avoid. Mortality is one of those truths. When someone accepts that life is temporary, wisdom deepens. Trivial frustrations lose power. Emotional energy is treated as valuable and finite, best spent on what matters.

This maturity influences everything. Relationships strengthen. Communication improves. Resilience grows. Conflict is handled with more grace. Acceptance of mortality becomes a turning point, not because it makes someone "serious" but because it makes someone clearer. Acknowledging the end helps people live with greater depth.

Reframing death can also reduce loneliness in grief. Many people feel alone in loss because they assume no one else thinks about death the way they do. They imagine others are untouched by the same fears or questions. That isolation intensifies grief.

But when families and communities treat death as a natural topic, loneliness begins to fade. People share memories. They speak fears aloud. They comfort one another without awkwardness. Shared understanding creates connection instead of isolation. Reframing death strengthens the social fabric that supports healing.

It also creates opportunities for legacy building. When someone sees death as part of life, they become more conscious of what they want to leave behind, not only possessions but values, stories, traditions, and emotional impact. They ask what imprint they want to make on family and community. They consider what wisdom they want children or grandchildren to carry forward.

This awareness often inspires action: recording memories, documenting lessons, writing letters, creating videos, sharing stories, mentoring others, becoming more intentional in relationships. Legacy becomes active instead of passive. Something shaped instead of left to chance. Reframing death creates space for someone to become a deliberate architect of their own legacy.

It also helps people live with less regret. Regret grows when important choices are postponed, words are left unsaid, apologies are never made, dreams are never pursued, planning is never completed. When death is seen as a natural transition rather than a distant event, people stop postponing what matters. They say what needs to be said. They take responsibility. They express love. They make amends. They pursue long-held goals.

Living with this awareness reduces regret because it encourages integrity and emotional alignment. People feel their days have meaning and that they are not leaving unfinished business behind. That reduction in regret enhances both life and the final chapter of it.

Reframing death also strengthens peace of mind. When death is feared, it feels like a shadow. When it is reframed, it becomes part of the landscape. It loses its power to intimidate. People feel calmer. More grounded. Hearts loosen. Sleep comes more easily. Life carries less tension.

Peace of mind grows when someone knows they have confronted what most people avoid. They have thought about the end. They have prepared for it. They have accepted it. That peace strengthens daily living. It creates emotional steadiness that touches every decision. Peace of mind is one of the greatest gifts that comes from reframing death.

Something else shifts as well: The desire to protect others becomes stronger. When someone fully understands mortality, instincts often change. People become more protective of the ones they love, not through fear but through responsibility. They want to leave guidance. They want to leave order. They want to leave comfort. They want to shield their family from hardship that does not need to exist.

This protective instinct becomes motivation to prepare. Planning stops being a task and becomes devotion. It becomes one of the clearest expressions of love a person can offer. Reframing death inspires a compassionate form of responsibility.

Ultimately, reframing death allows people to live with freedom. When someone is no longer running from the idea of death, a new lightness appears. They stop hiding from conversations that matter. They stop carrying the weight of denial. They feel more present, more connected, more alive.

They understand life is not defined only by length, but by quality. They see that preparing for the end deepens appreciation for the beginning and the middle. They find joy in ordinary moments, meaning in simple interactions, openness where fear used to live. Reframing death brings freedom that enhances the experience of being human.

Chapter 27

HOW TO BEGIN YOUR OWN JOURNEY TOWARD PREPAREDNESS

Many people hesitate to begin planning because they believe they need to understand everything first. They worry they are not knowledgeable enough, organized enough, or emotionally ready. But preparedness does not begin with expertise. It begins with willingness. A willingness to take a first small step. A willingness to look ahead with clear eyes. A willingness to protect the people you love.

Once willingness is present, the rest becomes far more approachable. Structure can be built. Knowledge can be learned. Support can be found. Tools exist to guide every stage. You do not need all the answers to begin. You only need the courage to start. Preparedness begins with a simple choice to move forward.

Most people imagine planning as overwhelming. They picture stacks of papers, endless forms, and hours of difficult conversations. That belief stops them before they begin. Yet in reality, the first step is usually a single action: writing down one wish, completing one document, or storing one important detail. The momentum that follows often feels natural. People discover each step is more manageable than expected. The process becomes less intimidating as progress builds. The mountain they imagined reveals itself to be a series of small, simple hills. Preparedness becomes approachable when people realize how gentle the first step can be.

Every planning journey begins differently because every person has different priorities. Some people start with end-of-life wishes because that feels most urgent. Some begin with a will because they want clarity for their family. Others start with legacy messages because they feel compelled to leave something meaningful. There is no single correct order. What matters most is momentum. Choosing the area that feels most important helps you move forward with energy and purpose. The rest can be added gradually. A journey built on personal values is easier to sustain than a journey built on obligation. Preparedness becomes meaningful when it begins with what matters most in the heart.

It also helps to allow the process to be emotional. Many people try to approach planning with pure logic, believing emotions will slow them down or complicate things. But planning touches memories, relationships, hopes, regrets, and love. It is normal for the process to bring tears, reflection, and unexpected feelings. Those emotions are not a problem. They are a sign the work matters. They clarify what you want and why you want it. They deepen understanding and strengthen resolve. When emotions are allowed rather than resisted, preparedness becomes a path toward self-awareness. Planning becomes richer when the heart is included.

One of the greatest barriers to preparedness is not knowing where to start, and this is where reliable tools matter. Guides, templates, checklists, and simple question-based platforms remove confusion and reduce mistakes. They make the path visible. Using tools does not weaken the planning process. It strengthens it by ensuring that essential details are not overlooked and by giving you confidence to continue. The right tools turn preparation into a guided journey rather than an overwhelming task.

Preparedness also becomes easier when you break it into manageable segments. You might begin with essential wishes. Then organize legal documents. Later list accounts and key information. After that, you may write legacy messages or record personal stories. Step by step, the structure builds. Each segment strengthens the next, and nothing needs to feel rushed. This rhythm prevents overwhelm and gives the mind time to process each part with clarity. The journey becomes achievable one clear segment at a time.

At some point, most people benefit from involving loved ones, but timing matters. Some prefer to begin privately. Others invite family in early. There is no single correct approach. What matters is that conversations happen when you are ready to share. When they do, loved ones often feel relief rather than discomfort. They feel honored to be trusted. These conversations reduce fear on all sides. They prevent future confusion. They strengthen emotional connection and create a sense of inclusion rather than secrecy. Preparedness deepens relationships when it is shared with care.

Another essential step is choosing a central, secure home for information. Scattered pieces create confusion. A single secure place creates order. This home may include wishes, legal documents, account lists, insurance details, legacy messages, and personal notes. When everything is stored together, the entire process becomes easier to manage and easier for loved ones to access when the time comes. Centralization brings peace of mind because it reduces the fear that something important will be lost or forgotten. Organization becomes a form of protection. A central home for information brings structure to the entire journey.

Preparedness is also not a one-time event. It is a living process. Wishes may change. Relationships evolve. New accounts are opened. New insights emerge. Periodic review keeps a plan aligned with the life you are living now. These updates do not require rebuilding everything. Small adjustments keep the structure accurate and relevant. This rhythm prevents outdated information from weakening the plan and ensures your loved ones will have the clearest guidance possible. A plan that evolves remains a source of comfort and accuracy.

Along the way, many people discover something unexpected: Preparedness is a gift to themselves as much as it is a gift to others. Many start out of love for their family, wanting to ease burdens, prevent conflict, and create order. But preparation also brings a sense of completion and emotional lightness. It clarifies values. It creates the feeling that your story is being held responsibly. It brings peace that sits quietly in the background of daily life. Preparedness strengthens both the one who prepares and the ones who will one day rely on those preparations.

It is also important to remember that you do not need to finish everything at once. People often pressure themselves to complete the entire planning process in one push, and that pressure creates unnecessary tension. Preparedness does not need to be rushed. It can unfold gradually. Each step adds stability. Each decision adds peace. Each completed segment builds confidence. Even partial progress can lift a tremendous emotional weight. When you accept that the journey can take time, you breathe more easily. You move at a sustainable pace. You reflect without urgency. Preparedness grows stronger with patience, and as you go, celebrate progress. Writing down one wish matters. Completing one document matters. Storing one account detail matters. These steps represent courage, clarity, and love. Recognizing progress reduces the heaviness people often associate with planning and reinforces motivation. It reminds you that preparedness is not only about the end of life; it is also about living with intention. Each accomplishment is evidence of growth and awareness, and celebration helps the journey continue.

In the end, preparedness is not separate from life. It reflects your values, relationships, priorities, and character. As you begin planning, you often see life with clearer eyes. You understand what you cherish most. You discover what you want your story to express. The plan and the life become interconnected. A well-prepared plan is a reflection of a well-examined life.

When the steps begin to come together, something powerful happens. You feel different— lighter, more grounded, more secure. You recognize that you have taken responsibility for something meaningful. Peace appears, not as a dramatic moment, but as a steady presence that comes when unfinished emotional responsibilities are finally addressed. That peace stays. It strengthens resilience. It deepens appreciation for life. Preparedness becomes not the end of a journey, but the beginning of a quieter, more confident way of living.

The journey toward preparedness is the journey toward peace.

Chapter 28

Living Fully and Leaving Wisely

Every person lives a story with a beginning, a middle, and an end. The end does not erase the beginning, and it does not overshadow the middle. It completes the arc. When people recognize this, they begin to see life differently. Each moment carries more depth. Each relationship gains more importance. Each decision holds more weight. Living fully is, in many ways, the decision to acknowledge finiteness rather than avoid it, because life becomes richer when we stop pretending it will last forever.

That awareness changes how people treat their days. They invest more intentionally in relationships. They honor their values instead of drifting from them. They make choices that reflect who they truly are rather than what is expected of them. They stop postponing what matters. They express love more freely. They forgive more often. They appreciate ordinary moments with renewed attention. Living fully begins with recognizing the preciousness of time.

Wisdom, of course, comes from living. It is shaped by trials, victories, failures, and the slow education of time. But wisdom also comes from preparing. There is a kind of insight that emerges when someone looks ahead with clarity and intention and decides to take responsibility for what will one day be left behind. Preparation teaches discipline. It teaches honesty. It teaches courage. It teaches self-awareness. It invites reflection not only on what has been experienced, but on the meaning someone hopes to leave in their wake. True wisdom is found in the combination: The lessons life gives us, and the responsibility we choose to carry.

Living fully also requires presence. Many people move through life at a pace that prevents them from noticing the very experiences that give their days meaning. They rush from one obligation to another. They focus on deadlines and pressures. They overlook the small moments that carry emotional significance. Living fully requires an intentional shift in attention. It means listening carefully when a loved one speaks. It means pausing long enough to appreciate simple joys. It means noticing the details that make life beautiful. It means valuing connection over distraction. It means approaching each day with gratitude rather than urgency. Presence enlarges life. It deepens relationships. It strengthens the heart.

Leaving wisely, then, is the natural companion to living fully. A wise departure is one that spares loved ones from unnecessary suffering. Not the suffering of grief, because grief is a natural expression of love, but the suffering created by confusion, unanswered questions, conflict, and disorganization. Leaving wisely means giving loved ones clarity, comfort, and guidance. It means documenting wishes. It means organizing essential information. It means creating a plan that allows the people who remain to move forward with confidence instead of fear. It means offering emotional safety at the moment they will need it most. Leaving wisely is one of the most compassionate choices a person can make.

Living fully also means embracing growth until the final day. Growth does not stop with age. It does not stop when responsibilities increase. It does not stop when life becomes complicated. Growth continues for as long as a person is willing to learn, reflect, improve, and adapt. Living fully requires a commitment to growth even when growth is uncomfortable.

It means learning from mistakes. It means strengthening relationships. It means becoming more patient, more present, more self-aware. It means evolving into the person you hope to be and allowing wisdom to guide actions rather than habit or fear. Growth is one of the clearest signs that someone is living with intention.

Leaving wisely also means accepting the reality of influence. Every person shapes the lives around them through words, choices, presence, absence, love, and silence. We influence one another in countless ways, and those effects do not stop when a life ends. Leaving wisely means acknowledging that influence and choosing to guide it with intention. It means understanding that what you do today will echo long after you are gone.

When someone prepares with care, they create a final influence rooted in peace rather than chaos. They offer direction instead of confusion and comfort instead of uncertainty. They leave behind a final gesture that says, "I cared for you enough to think ahead." That influence becomes part of the emotional inheritance of everyone who loved them. Wise preparation strengthens the generations that follow.

Living fully also means staying connected to what truly matters. People often drift from their deepest values without realizing it. Deadlines, errands, obligations, and noise can blur priorities until days begin to blend together. Living fully means returning again and again to the essentials: relationships, purpose, integrity, joy, service, gratitude. When someone reconnects with these values, life gains clarity, decisions become easier, stress loses power, meaning rises to the surface. That clarity influences both the present and the legacy being built. It enriches every chapter of life, and it steadies the mind when facing the final transition. Living fully means living aligned with what matters.

Leaving wisely also means creating space for healing. After a loss, loved ones need room to mourn. They need room to remember. They need room to process emotions that have no simple language. When someone leaves behind order instead of confusion, they create emotional breathing room. They remove barriers that would delay or complicate grief. They make it possible for family to move through sorrow with greater steadiness. This is one of the quietest and most powerful forms of love. Healing requires space. Preparation provides it. Leaving wisely nurtures the healing that follows loss.

Living fully also means accepting impermanence as a gift rather than a threat. Life moves in cycles. Seasons change. Children grow. Bodies age. Time passes whether we acknowledge it or not. Impermanence is one of the defining truths of existence. Many people fear it. Yet impermanence is also what gives beauty its intensity. Joy becomes sweeter because it does not last forever. Relationships become more meaningful because time together is limited. Life becomes richer because every moment is unique.

Accepting impermanence brings freedom. It allows people to appreciate the present moment rather than chase an illusion of permanence. It encourages generosity. It softens anger. It deepens love. When people embrace this truth, they live with humility and gratitude. Impermanence is not a threat. It is a reminder to cherish life.

Leaving wisely also means allowing loved ones to remember you with peace. The final memory someone leaves behind matters. It becomes part of future conversations, future holidays, and future family stories. When someone departs without preparation, loved ones often remember stress, confusion, and emotional struggle. Those memories linger and attach themselves to the legacy. But when clarity is left behind, loved ones remember steadiness. They remember care. They remember love expressed through action. They look back with gratitude rather than exhaustion. They feel guided rather than abandoned. That emotional imprint becomes part of how they heal and how they carry the story forward. Leaving wisely ensures that the final memory is one of peace.

Living fully also means offering love without delay. There is no guarantee of a perfect future moment to say the things that matter. No ideal time to express appreciation, repair a relationship, or share a memory. Living fully means offering love now. Speaking truth now. Giving kindness now. Showing gratitude now. These choices accumulate. They become the emotional foundation of a legacy. When love is expressed freely and consistently, it strengthens relationships and gives life depth. And later, those expressions become comfort that sustains the people who remain. Living fully means choosing love while there is still time.

Leaving wisely means ending with intention. An intentional ending honors the entire story that came before it. It acknowledges the relationships that shaped the journey. It preserves the values that guided a life. It ensures loved ones have what they need to move forward. It offers closure that feels aligned with character and identity. Intention transforms the final chapter from something feared into something meaningful. It becomes an act of love, courage, responsibility, and clarity. Leaving wisely is the final expression of a life lived with purpose.

This is why living fully and leaving wisely belong together. They are not separate paths. They strengthen each other. A person who lives fully becomes more aware of what they want to leave behind. A person who prepares thoughtfully becomes more present in everyday life. The two form a complete circle, purpose in the present, peace in what follows. To live fully is to embrace the beauty of each moment. To leave wisely is to protect the people who will remember those moments when you are gone. A well-lived life and a well-prepared departure form one of the truest expressions of love.

A Final Reflection for the Reader

Every person who reads this book has taken a courageous step. They have chosen to face a subject many avoid. They have chosen to reflect on their life and the lives of the people they love. They have chosen to think about responsibility and legacy. They have chosen growth over denial. This choice alone places them on a strong path.

The journey continues from here. It unfolds through honest conversations, thoughtful planning, and small intentional steps. It unfolds through clarity compassion and courage. It unfolds through living fully today while preparing wisely for tomorrow.

What matters most is not where a person begins but that they begin at all. The path toward peace is already open. The next step is yours to take.

Closing Note to the Reader

As you reach the end of this book, I want to acknowledge the significance of what you have just done. You spent time facing a part of life that most people avoid. You allowed yourself to explore difficult truths with honesty and courage. You walked through ideas that asked you to look at grief responsibility legacy and the emotional weight carried by those we love. That alone is meaningful. That alone is an act of maturity and compassion.

Throughout these chapters we explored the hidden layers of grief the stress that comes when families are unprepared and the peace that emerges when people take thoughtful steps ahead of time. We talked about love expressed through responsibility and the strength that grows when a person prepares, not because they expect the end but because they care about the living. We looked at the emotional costs of silence and the healing power of clarity. Together we reframed planning as something far greater than paperwork. It is a gift of stability, a gift of direction, a gift of comfort during one of the hardest moments a family will ever face.

Planning does not change the fact that life eventually ends. It changes everything about the experience for the people who remain. It gives them room to mourn. It lifts the weight of uncertainty. It preserves unity. It honors your identity. It allows the story of your life to be closed with intention instead of confusion. It brings peace when peace is needed most.

That is why I built *I Made the Arrangements*. I wanted to make this process easier for every person who understands the importance of leaving order rather than chaos. I wanted to create a place where your wishes could be documented where your information could be organized where your voice could be preserved and where your loved ones could find comfort instead of stress. I wanted to build something that reflects everything discussed in these pages. Something practical. Something compassionate. Something that gives families clarity when clarity matters more than anything else.

If this book has helped you see planning in a new light, then you have already taken an important step. The next steps do not have to be overwhelming. They can be gentle and gradual. Each piece you complete strengthens the path for your loved ones and brings peace to your own life.

Thank you for taking this journey. Thank you for being willing to reflect. Thank you for caring enough to plan. May the choices you make from here bring comfort to the people you love and may your life continue to be lived with intention meaning and wisdom.

www.ingramcontent.com/pod-product-compliance
Lightning Source LLC
LaVergne TN
LVHW011912080426
835508LV00007BA/490